THE TEACH EDUCATOR'S HANDBOOK

A narrative approach to professional learning

You might also like the following titles from Critical Publishing.

Becoming a Teacher Education Researcher
Edited by Diane Mayer and Ian Menter
ISBN: 9781913453299

Tackling Anxiety in Primary Mathematics Teachers
By Karen Wicks
ISBN: 9781913453015

Understanding Feedback: A critical exploration for teacher educators
By Caroline Elbra-Ramsay
ISBN: 9781913453251

Using Digital Video in Initial Teacher Education
By John McCullagh
ISBN: 9781913453336

Our titles are also available in a range of electronic formats. To order, or for details of our bulk discounts, please go to our website www.criticalpublishing.com or contact our distributor NBN International by telephoning 01752 202301 or emailing orders@nbninternational.com.

THE *TEACHER EDUCATOR'S HANDBOOK*

A narrative approach to professional learning

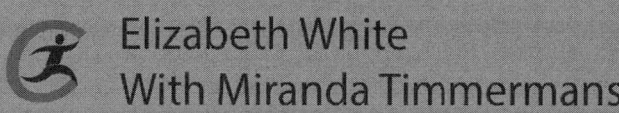

Elizabeth White
With Miranda Timmermans

First published in 2021 by Critical Publishing Ltd

All rights reserved. No part of this publication may be reproduced, stored in a retrieval system, or transmitted in any form or by any means, electronic, mechanical, photocopying, recording or otherwise, without prior permission in writing from the publisher.

The author has made every effort to ensure the accuracy of information contained in this publication, but assumes no responsibility for any errors, inaccuracies, inconsistencies and omissions. Likewise every effort has been made to contact copyright holders. If any copyright material has been reproduced unwittingly and without permission the Publisher will gladly receive information enabling them to rectify any error or omission in subsequent editions.

Copyright © (2021) Elizabeth White

British Library Cataloguing in Publication Data
A CIP record for this book is available from the British Library

ISBN: 978-1-913453-65-7

This book is also available in the following e-book formats:
EPUB: 978-1-913453-67-1
Adobe e-book reader: 978-1-913453-68-8

The right of Elizabeth White to be identified as the Author of this work has been asserted by her in accordance with the Copyright, Design and Patents Act 1988.

Cover and text design by Greensplash Limited
Project management by Newgen Publishing UK
Printed and bound in Great Britain by 4edge, Essex

Critical Publishing
3 Connaught Road
St Albans
AL3 5RX

www.criticalpublishing.com

Paper from responsible sources

CONTENTS

	Acknowledgements	vi
	About the author	vii
	List of abbreviations, figures and tables	viii
	Foreword	ix
	Preface	x
Chapter 1	Introduction	1
Chapter 2	Guiding and assessing students	12
Chapter 3	Working collaboratively	24
Chapter 4	Professionalism and well-being	33
Chapter 5	Quality of provision	46
Chapter 6	Using the stories collaboratively	57
Chapter 7	Your own stories about practice	66
Chapter 8	Using the stories creatively	72
	Glossary	77
	Appendix: List of teacher educator stories	78
	Index	79

ACKNOWLEDGEMENTS

Firstly, I would like to thank Dr Miranda Timmermans of Avans University of Applied Sciences, Breda, the Netherlands, for a long and fruitful research collaboration focusing on the professional development of teacher educators working in partnerships in initial teacher education. As chair of Velon, the Dutch Association of Teacher Educators, Miranda brings an understanding of the complexities of partnership work across the Netherlands. We were struck from the first that partnership work 'on the ground' was not only our shared focus as practitioners and researchers, but was also the key to effective teacher education and that there was a need for professional development resources for teacher educators to use to learn both independently and collaboratively, to enrich their practice.

Miranda and I would like to thank all the teachers and teacher educators who have contributed to our research directly, sharing their stories of challenges in practice, and those who have contributed their ideas of how to use the stories for the professional development of teacher educators. We are grateful to those who have influenced us while we have been working collaboratively on initial and continuing professional development programmes.

I am also grateful to Dr Claire Dickerson for her tireless help and encouragement throughout the research and beyond, to the writing of this handbook. Thank you to Nicki Rooke, SCITT director at Alban Federation, for her helpful review of the text and for providing the foreword to introduce the book. Thank you also to Professor Joy Jarvis, Vicky Pateman, and my wonderful colleagues in the School of Education, who are an inspiration to me. Finally, I express my gratitude to Julia Morris at Critical Publishing, and her colleagues, for their guidance in the production of this handbook. I hope that you will be stimulated in your thinking as you develop your professional practice both personally and within and between your institutions.

ABOUT THE **AUTHOR**

ELIZABETH WHITE

Elizabeth White worked in employment-based initial teacher training for the Hertfordshire Regional Partnership while being employed as a secondary science teacher. In 2009 the provision was graded as outstanding by the Office for Standards in Education, Children's Services and Skills (Ofsted). She was involved in setting up the School Direct Programme in the School of Education at the University of Hertfordshire, England, where she is in the leadership team supporting the development of teacher educators in schools and the university. Her research has included self-study of her experience as a new teacher educator, developing a new aspect to her identity and research-rich pedagogical practice. She is currently researching how to effectively develop quality teacher education within partnerships. Elizabeth is co-chair of the Professional Development of Teacher Educators Research and Development Community of the Association for Teacher Education in Europe and secretary of the International Professional Development Association (England).

MIRANDA TIMMERMANS

This book has been written in co-operation with Miranda Timmermans, who works as a researcher (applied professor) at Avans University of Applied Sciences, Breda, the Netherlands. She leads the research group 'Leerkracht', who research school-based teacher education and workplace learning and teaching of (future) teachers. Her PhD was on the quality of Professional Development Schools (teaching schools). Although she still is engaged in the quality question, her research and work are now focused on workplace learning and teaching and school-based teacher education – trying to find critical characteristics of a workplace pedagogy. Miranda is chair of a committee which assesses newly started partnerships (commissioned by the government – Department of Education). She guides new partnerships for the school-based teacher education platform, develops materials for professional development and is involved in developing a peer review system and assessment criteria for monitoring the development of partnership work. Miranda is also the chair of Velon, the Dutch Association of Teacher Educators. The aim of Velon is to contribute to the quality of teacher educators and of the profession.

ABBREVIATIONS, FIGURES AND TABLES

Abbreviations

DfE	Department for Education
FLiTE	For Learning in Teacher Education
IBTE	university- or institute-based teacher educator
ITE	initial teacher education
ITT	initial teacher training
NASBTT	National Association of School-Based Teacher Trainers
SBTE	school-based teacher educator
TEMZ	Teacher Educator and Mentoring Zone

Figures

3.1	Building collaboration	27

Tables

1.1	Themes and subthemes found within the stories	5
6.1	The stories cross-referenced to the Mentor Standards	61
8.1	Some ways to use the stories	73
9.1	Glossary of terms	77

FOREWORD

When I was invited to interview for the post of director of the Alban Federation School-Centred Initial Teacher Training (SCITT) provision in October 2019, I was asked to deliver a presentation to headteachers on what I perceived to be the challenges in initial teacher education (ITE) over the next three years. While preparing my answers, I couldn't help but revisit the concept that in every challenge lies opportunity. The current time is certainly proving to be one of the most challenging and changing landscapes the education sector has ever faced, and yet, as a teacher educator who has been involved in the development of early career teachers for well over a decade, I'm excited about the prospects for developing and strengthening ITE. The Core Content Framework, Early Career Framework and two-year induction period for newly qualified teachers have been introduced to provide the vital support and training new teachers need to thrive. The role of teacher educator has always been crucial, but now is an ideal opportunity to re-evaluate our practice and consider how best we can implement high-quality professional development. This will enable teacher educators in both schools and universities to encourage and inspire those new to the profession to grow and thrive to become the best teachers they can be.

While resources are becoming readily available to support new teachers through this early period of professional development, there are very few resources that are designed specifically for the development of teacher educators and can be used individually or in partnerships to invite and enhance the critical conversations that need to take place surrounding practice. This handbook takes an alternative approach to sharing experiences across the sector. Through the collection of real stories, it facilitates the dissemination of good practice, professional debate and empathy for all the various parties involved in training the teachers of tomorrow. I was fortunate enough to attend a workshop held by Liz White and Miranda Timmermans early in their research. The dialogues prompted from the early stories collated in the project have had a lasting impact on my own professional development. As a facilitator, Liz was open to the various and sometimes conflicting feedback, she demonstrated unwavering positivity in her prompting of coaching questions, and above all else was authentic in her passion to support teacher educators through her research and relatable case studies.

The stories in this handbook could easily be used by initial teacher education providers during mentor training workshops. There is an omission of right and wrong approaches, with the focus instead being placed clearly on personal reflection: this would create a dynamic training dialogue. Equally, the stories could be used by school-based teacher educators as part of in-house training. In my previous role as a professional mentor in school, with a large cohort of student teachers each year, I would ask for time on school INSET days to meet with the mentors and undertake a short training task. The stories in this handbook would provide excellent resources for such in-house training.

At a time when there have been significant disruptions to teacher training along with major shifts in school life, this resource is needed now more than ever.

Nicki Rooke, SCITT director at Alban Federation

PREFACE

This handbook has been written to meet a need for professional development resources to support the professional learning of teacher educators. It is 'For Learning in Teacher Education' and links closely with the FLiTE platform (www.go.herts.ac.uk/FLiTE).

The handbook models a narrative approach to professional learning that can easily be translated into the work of a teacher educator in leading the professional learning of others. The stories provided are embedded in the practice of teacher educators working in partnerships. They give different stakeholders in these partnerships an opportunity to stand in each other's shoes and to see practice from a different perspective. So often we have good intentions behind our practice, but when we seek to implement these intentions, they do not have the impact we were anticipating. Somehow things get 'lost in translation' from policy level in partnerships to the experience 'on the ground'. By examining the critical incidents that arise in our practice and cause us friction, we can start to unpick what is actually happening, opening up our practice for reflection, discussion and development.

Through using insightful stories of challenges in practice written by teacher educators working in schools and universities, teacher educators can experience the benefits of using a narrative approach to professional learning. The handbook is designed as a tool for teacher educators, provoking discussion to support collaborative working practices, explore new possibilities and enhance the quality of school-based teacher education. It also provides practical support to help teacher educators to grow and work on their own professional development. The stories and critical questions in each chapter can support the professional learning of teacher educators in both schools and universities, enabling their different contributions to be better understood and valued. They can be used within schools, universities and partnerships, with teacher educators from both settings, and with others involved in initial teacher education including those supervising initial teacher education, mentors, students, school leaders, and managers of initial teacher education.

FLiTE (For Learning in Teacher Education) is a platform where those involved in initial teacher education can find resources and inspiration to develop their practice. It is designed by teacher educators, for teacher educators to:

- » inspire critical reflection on school-based practice in teacher education;
- » deepen the professional learning and development of teacher educators;
- » develop collaborative working in initial teacher education partnerships;
- » enhance the quality of learning opportunities for students.

The stories and critical questions in this handbook are available as downloadable resources on the FLiTE website.

This handbook and the FLiTE website arise from our research investigating the experiences, emerging roles and professional development needs of school-based teacher educators (SBTEs) and those working in partnership with them. Our focus on this complex role provides new insights as much current literature relates to institute-based teacher educators (IBTEs). Experienced teachers becoming teacher educators need to be situated within a professional learning community with experienced teacher educators, to develop their emerging identity as a teacher educator and an understanding of the professional knowledge and practice of teacher educators. This is essential in sustainable models of teacher education.

The stories are also available in Dutch in *The Great Storybook*, on the Platform Samen Opleiden and Professionaliseren: www.platformsamenopleiden.nl/groteverhalenboek/

CHAPTER 1 | INTRODUCTION

Focusing on practice 'on the ground'

The idea of providing evidence for 'what works' has been a dominant discourse in educational research and practice. The focus is on simple generalisable solutions to complex challenges faced in practice. We also need to ask 'what should it work for?', that is, what is the purpose of our work; and 'what works for whom?', that is, who should be involved in deciding the purpose (Biesta, 2007). If you are looking for quick fixes, or 'top tips', this handbook is not for you! Instead, by focusing on particular issues in practice, through a narrative approach, this handbook will help to provide you with an interpretive space to provoke your reflective engagement with the daily dilemmas we experience in school-based initial teacher education. This approach offers us an opportunity for professional development that expands our understanding of the workplace and the participants in initial teacher education and retunes our practice for the current context in which we are working. As we come to the stories of teacher educators' experiences, we need to be open to influence and to be careful not to shut down interpretation or to rush and over-simplify. This in turn will enable us to be open to exploring pedagogy and practice, and to developing our own potential. In attempting to answer the legitimate question of 'what works?', we must not take away the possibility of educational judgement and reflection from the one asking the question (Korsgaard, 2020).

Teacher educators and their professional development

In this handbook we are using the following broad definition for teacher educators:

Teacher educators are all those who have a formal active role in the facilitation of professional learning by student teachers and teachers. They may be workplace-based or university-based. In some cases they may specialise in pedagogy or in the teaching of a specific curriculum subject.

(Boyd and White, 2017, p 126)

This inclusive definition embraces teacher educators who are school-based (SBTEs) or university- (or institute-based, IBTEs). Within school, some teacher educators may be working as mentors, alongside students or early career teachers, on a daily basis, while others have a supervisory role for all students within their schools and/or responsibility for the professional development of all teaching staff.

The current context of learning to teach in England, as in many developed countries, is complex and evolving. The world around us is altering exponentially due to the impact of the Covid-19 pandemic, the pace of technological transformation, the impact of environmental change and the rise in attention on social justice. There is increased uncertainty about the future, job insecurity, and anxiety about health, leading to an unprecedented focus on our well-being and mental health. Within schools, there is a more diverse population of pupils due to migration and an increased emphasis on using practices that are rigorously underpinned by research evidence from randomised controlled trials (see for example www.educationendowmentfoundation.org.uk/). There are challenges in retaining teachers, who are grappling with challenging workloads and constant change. Initial teacher education has become a focus of many governments, bringing with it increasing policy demands regarding an increased focus on school-based experience to develop practice; increased expectations for schools to take responsibility in teacher education; and more regulation regarding the curriculum that students have an entitlement to. This has led to a shift in the roles of IBTEs and SBTEs, and more complexity in the way that they work together in partnerships. If ever there was a need for careful consideration of the professional development needs of teacher educators, it is now! Approaching these changes in our working context with a positive mindset can provoke professional growth and development.

The roles, identity and professional development of IBTEs have been the focus of a growing body of research (Lunenberg et al, 2007; Czerniawski et al, 2017; van der Klink et al, 2017), while those of SBTEs, and the way that IBTEs and SBTEs develop their practice working in school–university partnerships, have not received the same attention. SBTEs have a valuable and vital, but not well-recognised, role in teacher education. There is a need to provide for their professional learning in collaboration with the wider teacher educator community (Westrup and Jackson, 2009; White et al, 2015; Andreasen et al, 2019). This need has been one of the motivations behind this handbook. Developing mentors often puts pressure on schools with regard to release time. In England, the length of mandatory induction of new teachers is increasing to two years with a requirement for mentoring during this period. This will be an additional challenge for schools. SBTEs can use the stories in this handbook in-house with the mentors in their schools to support their development, choosing an appropriate theme to match the context and challenges they are facing.

Why stories?

Korsgaard (2020) argues that we become skilled in our professional and practical judgement through developing practical wisdom through learning from the practice of other professionals, and continually reflecting on our pedagogy. He proposes the use of examples; although examples do not provide certain solutions, they are communicable. Examples can take many forms, of which our stories of practice are one. An advantage of using storytelling is that it involves communicating in a different way that allows the language to be easier to understand (Jarvis, 2005). This contrasts with scenarios that may be created with a specific purpose in mind and tend to describe aspects of practice in an objective and precise way, deliberately drawing in points that the author wants us to notice, while taking a less personal perspective. Teacher educators are more likely to identify with stories, relating to the narrative voice of the author and even finding their place among the characters within.

Storytelling is a narrative approach, based on the premise that the ways in which teachers think about education is embedded in the stories they tell each other and themselves (Carter, 1993). Stories have a certain shape, involving a before, something happening, and an after. When we read stories, we can project our personal values and experience onto the content (Scholes, 1980). So, we find that others interpret stories differently from us. For example, when a group of teacher educators read a story of a challenge in practice written by another teacher educator, often they each give the story a different title that brings out an element within the story that they relate to particularly on that day, because of their experiences and their current context.

Stories of challenges in practice can capture the complexities of practice 'on the ground' in initial teacher education partnerships, where there are many stakeholders working, some of whom are crossing boundaries between institutions where there are different priorities and different ethos. Interpretation may be ambiguous, which can provide more freedom to explore different possible solutions (White et al, 2020b). They also help us to articulate our practice and examine our beliefs, and to surface strategies used to manage inconsistencies between beliefs and practice (Tillema and Kremer-Hayon, 2005). The stories in this handbook were written by teacher educators for teacher educators and provide authentic teacher educator voices for professional learning. They may trigger a discussion and examination of beliefs around school-based practice when they are employed as professional learning and development tools for teacher educators working individually or collaboratively.

Where did the stories come from?

The stories were collected from teacher educators working in school-based initial teacher education partnerships in the Netherlands and England. Both countries have experienced a move to increase the role of schools in initial teacher education. In the Netherlands, school–university partnerships have co-responsibility for 'Opleiden in de school' where new teachers learn by participating in genuine teaching practices (Ten Dam and Blom, 2006, p 649). In England, School Direct routes into teaching (DfE, 2010, 2011) have expanded school-led teacher education. There is increased time in the workplace in both countries, so teacher educators must take advantage of the school context to enhance professional learning (van Velzen and Timmermans, 2014).

In initial teacher education, IBTEs are usually responsible for teaching students about teaching, nurturing their reflective practice and development as a teacher, and quality assuring the programme overall. SBTEs usually co-ordinate the professional development of teachers in their school, supervising students' school-based experience, and liaising with the university. They are also taking on more responsibility for quality assurance of teacher education within their schools or alliances. SBTEs are responsible for co-assessing students in the Netherlands, while in England they may be responsible for assessing students, while IBTEs verify or moderate student assessment. Practice in initial teacher education is evolving, so SBTEs and IBTEs need to learn new ways of working collaboratively, which needs to be considered in planning professional development opportunities for teacher educators (White et al, 2020b). At this point it is also important to note that the roles of IBTEs and SBTEs within a partnership may be clearly defined, as in the Netherlands (Velon, 2012) or more ambiguous (Mason, 2013). In England, many terms are used for the different stakeholders in initial teacher education (see Glossary), and each partnership may distribute the roles of these key professionals in different ways. The term SBTE may incorporate teacher mentors who support the day-to-day development of students as well as those who co-ordinate and supervise all the school-based training within their school.

A total of 35 stories were collected for an international research project, the aim of which was to explore the professional learning of teacher educators by asking them about their challenges or dilemmas while working in partnerships, and how they resolve them (White et al, 2020a). Teacher educators were asked to write a brief story about a specific challenge or dilemma that they had faced in their recent practice. They were asked to include a beginning, a plot, and an ending (if there was one!). The following questions were provided as prompts.

> » *What was the real challenge for you?*
> » *Where did the challenge arise?*
> » *How did you deal with it?*
> » *How did that work?*

More information about collecting stories of practice is given in Chapter 7. Some of the stories about challenges in practice were shared with teacher educators in workshops in both England and the Netherlands and at international conferences, in order to consider ways in which they could enable institutional boundary crossing in partnerships. These ideas were then used to develop 'tools' for the professional learning and development of teacher educators. The tools were trialled and evaluated for their usefulness for professional learning and development. They were found to be helpful, especially when used with SBTEs and IBTEs together (White et al, 2020b). The tools and other web-based resources are available in English and Dutch for the international teacher educator community. The Appendix contains a table of the teacher educator stories within this book, which are cross-referenced with the FLiTE resources.

For Learning in Teacher Education

Website: www.go.herts.ac.uk/FLiTE

Twitter: @FLiTE737

Email: FLiTE@herts.ac.uk

The stories are also available in Dutch in *The Great Storybook*, on the Platform Samen Opleiden and Professionaliseren: www.platformsamenopleiden.nl/groteverhalenboek/

How to use this handbook

Each chapter contains the following sections.

Key themes

Four themes emerged from the thematic analysis of the stories (White et al, 2020a), which were divided into subthemes. Table 1.1 provides an example to illustrate each subtheme that was identified in the research. This demonstrates the kinds of challenges being faced 'on the ground' by teacher educators working in initial teacher education partnerships. The four themes are covered in Chapters 2 to 5, with stories selected from some of the subthemes.

Table 1.1 Themes and subthemes found within the stories

	Number of incidences	**Example**
Guiding and assessing students	35; in 28 of 35 stories	
Assessment (judgements around pass or fail)	11	Dutch IBTE in primary: preparing for a conversation with a student regarding failing their assessment
Guiding students' teaching	13	English SBTE in secondary: supporting a teacher mentor in guiding the students' learning and judicious assessment of their progress
Providing learning opportunities for students	5	Dutch SBTE in a vocational setting: helping students to learn from their workplace experiences
Teaching students	6	English SBTE in secondary: working with students who were not engaged with the learning
Working collaboratively	18; in 15 of 35 stories	
Communication in partnership	4	Dutch SBTE in a vocational setting: dealing with communication at all levels between the university and the school
Working in partnership across institutions	11	Dutch IBTE in secondary: working with a group of SBTEs who are not readily co-operating with the university
Working with school leadership	1	Dutch SBTE in a vocational setting: coaching a good student and colleague with no support in the end from the head/director
Roles of teacher educators in the partnership	2	Dutch SBTE in a vocational setting: working together with the IBTE – having double role of assessing and coaching

Table 1.1 (*Cont.*)

	Number of incidences	Example
Professionalism and well-being	14; in 10 of 35 stories	
Professionalism (teacher educator)	3	Dutch IBTE in secondary: helping a student to move on after a difficult issue within a school
Professionalism (student)	4	English SBTE in secondary: working with a critical student who alienates other members of staff
Personal growth and identity (teacher educator)	1	Dutch SBTE in primary: facing tensions in taking on the role of SBTE
Personal growth and identity (student)	4	Dutch IBTE in secondary: coaching a student who is not afforded the rich learning environment needed
Well-being (student)	2	English SBTE in secondary: responding to signs of a mental health issue in a student
Quality of provision	5; in 5 of 35 stories	
Quality assurance	3	English SBTE in secondary: choosing to change the mentor to support a student to make progress
Training for co-ordinating SBTEs	1	Dutch SBTE in primary: tensions in teaching colleagues to coach students on reflection
Mentor training	1	Dutch SBTE in primary: improving mentor training, using feedback from mentors and giving mentors a voice

Teacher educator stories

It is best to approach each story without a preconceived idea of what the story is about, and to ask yourself the question 'what is this story about?' There is no right or wrong answer, but the answer will be related to where you are at in your own professional development, the context in which you are working locally and nationally, and your past experience.

If you are using a story collaboratively, then you will find a richness from sharing the story and finding out what each person in the group thinks it is about. Often other teacher educators will highlight something different from the story, if you listen carefully to what they are saying. This, in itself, provides the opportunity for learning from each other.

Some stories can be used well when paired together, for example Stories 5.2 and 5.3, which are two different approaches to the same challenge around mentoring. The stories do not provide 'the' answer to the challenge being faced as there are often many ways that the challenges can be resolved. By considering the two different approaches taken, it is possible to consider a variety of actions and when which action might be most appropriate. This may look different depending on whether you are based in the school where the student is working or if you are based at the university or central base of the partnership.

Critical questions

Each story is followed by critical questions that you may like to use. However, you may have critical questions of your own, relating to the central theme that you identified as relevant to you within the story.

Many of the critical questions can be used as activities in collaborative professional development across boundaries. You may find the critical questions from one of the other stories work just as well with this story for you, as they are designed to provoke your thinking. They were developed as activities from ideas provided when working with groups of teacher educators exploring the stories. At the end of any activity, ask what you have learnt from the story and what you have learnt through using the activity. When you are working in a group with the stories, make sure you set aside time to share this learning with the group, as it can provide deeper reflection and appreciation of how you and your colleagues learn professionally.

Coaching questions

Towards the end of each chapter, there are thought-provoking coaching questions which can be used in a number of ways to develop practice. For example, a professional mentor in school could use the questions to coach a new mentor; a visiting tutor from a university could use them to coach a new professional mentor or teacher mentor; or mentors could use them in peer mentoring pairings.

Reflections

Looking back on the stories and challenges in each chapter provides reflective learning. You might like to note your own reflections before reading this section, as drawing together your understanding through writing a synopsis and linking it with your reading is a valuable form of professional development, helping you to embed your learning.

Further resources and references

Each chapter ends with a list of further resources with detailed descriptions of what is available from these different organisations, reports, books and websites. You may find these especially useful if you are working towards a higher degree or other recognition for your educational leadership. A full list of references is also provided at the end of each chapter.

Individual or collaborative professional development?

You can work through this handbook using each of the stories and critical questions individually to support your own professional learning and develop your thinking using the further resources and references.

Alternatively, you can use the stories and critical questions as group activities. The stories were originally developed into tools for collaborative professional learning to enable institutional boundary crossing in partnerships.

In Chapter 6 we explore 'using the stories collaboratively' within a partnership, in a setting or across institutional boundaries, or with teacher educators from different partnerships. Exploring the stories together with colleagues can facilitate useful discussions to help disseminate good practice around challenging aspects of practice currently being experienced. The stories can support curriculum and leadership development. They can be used in relation to the Mentor Standards (DfE, 2016) and other professional frameworks for teacher educators to enable professional learning and development.

Chapter 7 looks at exploring 'your own stories about practice' with guidance on how to write stories; how to support others in writing their stories about practice; and different tools to help you reflect on stories about practice that you or your colleagues have written.

Additional ways to use the stories are included in Chapter 8, about 'using the stories creatively'. A wide variety of ideas have been collected from teacher educators in workshops when they have been introduced to the stories and have explored possible ways to use them. Here you can also consider how you might use this narrative approach more widely in your own practice, to support the professional learning of others.

> **REFLECTIONS**
>
> Reviewing the aspects of practice that teacher educators in initial teacher education partnerships are finding challenging, we may feel that these challenges have not changed over the years. However, it is important to remember that different teacher educators are facing these challenges due to a shift in responsibilities within partnerships in response to the increasing role of schools in teacher education. The professional development of teacher educators has been neglected in many countries, which may mean that professional knowledge may not be readily accessed by new teacher educators (European Commission, 2013; InFo-TED, '2019). There has been a lack of specific induction for new teacher educators, with many holding the mistaken belief that all teachers can be teacher educators, or that the professional knowledge of teachers and teacher educators is the same. However, teacher educators have a different professional knowledge base from teachers, and attention needs to be paid to their professional development needs (Swennen, 2014).

> In looking at these stories, we are seeking a different type of learning from the challenges – not easy answers and solutions and 'tips' to pass on to others, but ways of developing the characteristics required to be a teacher educator. These are not easily learnt and come through a lifetime of learning deeply from experience. Using a narrative approach for professional development can involve this kind of transformative learning, leading to resilience for changing educational landscapes (Jarvis, 2005). There is always more to learn from the challenges we experience in practice, and a deeper level to explore, because our work is relational, situated in complex partnerships that span institutional borders and with multiple stakeholders involved. Sometimes these challenges do not need to be resolved, but rather need to be explored and learnt from. Some are not resolved because they are beyond the control of the teacher educator 'on the ground' and may need to be dealt with on a different level within the partnership. If a solution is needed, what is important is who should be involved in working out the solution.

Further resources

InFo-TED. [online] Available at: https://info-ted.eu/ (accessed 6 February 2021).

InFo-TED is an international forum working to promote professional development of teacher educators. It aims to build an interactive network of European teacher educators to learn from each other via a virtual learning platform and face-to-face meetings; create resources to support the professional development of teacher educators; and foster knowledge creation and a shared European vision for teacher educator development and teacher educator leadership. The blog https://info-ted.eu/blog/ provides reflective accounts of teacher educators' practice.

National Association of School-Based Teacher Trainers (NASBTT). [online] Available at: www.nasbtt.org.uk/ (accessed 6 February 2021).

Members of NASBTT can register to access the Teacher Educator and Mentoring Zone (TEMZ) dedicated to supporting the professional learning and development of teacher educators individually and as a profession. The resources in this zone are organised by the *Professional Framework for Teacher Educators* into four themes: professional learning and development; learning and teaching; professional relationships; and organise and manage.

References

Andreasen, J K, Bjørndal, C R P and Kovač, V B (2019) Being a Teacher and Teacher Educator: The Antecedents of Teacher Educator Identity among Mentor Teachers. *Teaching and Teacher Education*, 85: 281–91. https://doi.org/https://doi.org/10.1016/j.tate.2019.05.011

Biesta, G (2007) Why "What Works" Won't Work: Evidence-based Practice and the Democratic Deficit in Educational Research. *Educational Theory*, 57(1): 1–22. https://doi.org/10.1111/j.1741-5446.2006.00241.x

Boyd, P and White, E (2017) Teacher Educator Professional Inquiry in an Age of Accountability. In Boyd, P and Szplit, A (eds) *Teachers and Teacher Educators Learning Through Inquiry: International Perspectives*. Kraków: Attyka. [online] Available at: http://researchprofiles.herts.ac.uk/portal/files/12126690/Teacher_Educator_Professional_Inquiry_in_an_Age_of_Accountability._Boyd_White_2017.pdf (accessed 6 February 2021).

Carter, K (1993) The Place of Story in the Study of Teaching and Teacher Education. *Educational Researcher*, 22: 5–18. https://doi.org/10.3102/0013189X022001005

Czerniawski, G, Guberman, A and MacPhail, A (2017) The Professional Developmental Needs of Higher Education-Based Teacher Educators: An International Comparative Needs Analysis. *European Journal of Teacher Education*, 40(1): 127–40. https://doi.org/10.1080/02619768.2016.1246528

Department for Education (DfE) (2010) *The Importance of Teaching: The Schools White Paper 2010.* [online] Available at: www.gov.uk/government/publications/the-importance-of-teaching-the-schools-white-paper-2010 (accessed 12 March 2021).

Department for Education (DfE) (2011) *Training Our Next Generation of Outstanding Teachers.* [online] Available at: www.gov.uk/government/publications/training-our-next-generation-of-outstanding-teachers-an-improvement-strategy-for-discussion (accessed 12 March 2021).

Department for Education (DfE) (2016) *National Standards for School-Based Initial Teacher Training (ITT) Mentors.* [online] Available at: https://assets.publishing.service.gov.uk/government/uploads/system/uploads/attachment_data/file/536891/Mentor_standards_report_Final.pdf (accessed 12 March 2021).

European Commission (2013) *Supporting Teacher Educators for Better Learning Outcomes.* [online] Available at: https://ec.europa.eu/assets/eac/education/policy/school/doc/support-teacher-educators_en.pdf (accessed 6 February 2021).

InFo-TED (2019) *The Importance of Teacher Educators: Professional Development Imperatives.* White paper. [online] Available at: https://info-ted.eu/wp-content/uploads/2019/10/InFo-TED-White-Paper.pdf (accessed 6 February 2021).

Jarvis, J (2005) Telling Stories in Class: An Exploration of Aspects of the Use of Narrative in a Higher Education Context. *Journal for the Enhancement of Learning and Teaching*, 2(1): 6–13. [online] Available at: https://uhra.herts.ac.uk/handle/2299/2582 (accessed 6 February 2021).

Korsgaard, M T (2020) Exemplarity and Education: Retuning Educational Research. *British Educational Research Journal*, 46(6): 1357–70. https://doi.org/10.1002/berj.3636

Lunenberg, M, Korthagen, F and Swennen, A (2007) The Teacher Educator as a Role Model. *Teaching and Teacher Education*, 23: 586–601. https://doi.org/10.1016/j.tate.2006.11.001

Mason, K O (2013) Teacher Involvement in Pre-service Teacher Education. *Teachers and Teaching*, 19(5): 559–74. https://doi.org/10.1080/13540602.2013.827366

Scholes, R (1980) Language, Narrative, and Anti-narrative. *Critical Inquiry*, 7(1): 204–12. https://doi.org/10.1086/448096

Swennen, A (2014) More Than 'Just' a Teacher: The Identity of Teacher Educators. In Jones, K and White, E (eds) *Developing Outstanding Practice in School-Based Teacher Education*. Northwich: Critical Publishing.

Ten Dam, G T and Blom, S (2006) Learning Through Participation. The Potential of School-based Teacher Education for Developing a Professional Identity. *Teaching and Teacher Education*, 22: 647–60. https://doi.org/10.1016/j.tate.2006.03.003

Tillema, H and Kremer-Hayon, L (2005) Facing Dilemmas: Teacher-Educators' Ways of Constructing a Pedagogy of Teacher Education. *Teaching in Higher Education*, 10(2): 203–17. https://doi.org:10.1080/1356251042000337954

Van der Klink, M, Kools, Q, Avissar, G, White, S and Sakata, T (2017) Professional Development of Teacher Educators: What Do They Do? Findings from an Explorative International Study. *Professional Development in Education*, 43(2): 163–78. https://doi.org/10.1080/19415257.2015.1114506

van Velzen, C and Timmermans, M (2014) What Can We Learn from the Shift Towards a More School-Centred Model in the Netherlands? In Jones, K and White, E (eds) *Developing Outstanding Practice in School-Based Teacher Education*. Northwich: Critical Publishing.

Velon (2012) Professional Standard for Teacher Educators. [online] Available at: https://velon.nl/beroepsregistratie/beroepsstandaard/ (accessed 6 February 2021).

Westrup, R and Jackson, A (2009) Professional Development Needs of Teacher Educators in Higher Education Institutions (HEIs) and School-Based Mentors in Schools. [online] Available at: www.heacademy.ac.uk/knowledge-hub/professional-development-needs-teacher-educators-higher-education-institutions-heis (accessed 6 February 2021).

White, E, Dickerson, C and Weston, K (2015) Developing an Appreciation of What It Means to be a School-Based Teacher Educator. *European Journal of Teacher Education*, 38(4): 445–59. https://doi.org/10.1080/02619768.2015.1077514

White, E, Timmermans, M and Dickerson, C (2020a) Learning from Professional Challenges Identified by School and Institute-Based Teacher Educators within the Context of School–University Partnership. *European Journal of Teacher Education*, 1–17. https://doi.org/10.1080/02619768.2020.1803272

White, E, Timmermans, M and Dickerson, C (2020b) Learning from Stories about the Practice of Teacher Educators in Partnerships between Schools and Higher Education Institutions. In Swennen, A and White, E (eds) *Being a Teacher Educator: Research-Informed Methods for Improving Practice*. London: Routledge.

CHAPTER 2 | GUIDING AND ASSESSING STUDENTS

KEY **THEMES**

This chapter is about:
- *guiding students' teaching;*
- *providing learning opportunities for students;*
- *assessment (judgements around pass/fail).*

TEACHER EDUCATOR **STORIES**

Teacher educator story 2.1 is written by a school-based teacher educator about assessing a student.

Teacher educator story 2.2 is written by an institute-based teacher educator about providing opportunities for students in school.

Teacher educator story 2.3 is written by a school-based teacher educator about supporting a student to make progress.

Developing your initial teacher education curriculum

Providing equal opportunity for students learning in school is a vital consideration for partnerships. Every workplace will be different, and every student has different prior knowledge and professional learning needs. Although experiences will be very different, there will be a common set of learning objectives for students, arising from the initial teacher education curriculum that the partnership has developed. In England this will include coverage of the *ITT Core Content Framework* (DfE, 2019). It is important that the formal teaching of students and their school-based learning are carefully and explicitly linked to enable students to understand the underpinning rationale for decisions about practice. There also needs to be an understanding within the partnership of where the responsibility lies for different aspects of the curriculum, as partnerships must ensure that students have access to the full entitlement of foundational knowledge and skills defined in the core framework, or other national equivalent. In designing the curriculum, partnerships need to carefully construct learning opportunities and teaching into a coherent sequence that supports students to succeed in the classroom. Stories of challenges in practice can be used to develop curriculum design by providing stimulation for thinking about the shared vision for the outcome of the programme in terms of the kind of teachers that are being prepared and the unique contributions of all the expert colleagues (professionals including experienced and effective teachers, subject specialists, mentors and tutors) working with the student.

The pedagogy of teacher education has its own unique considerations. The initial teacher education curriculum may explicitly contain the content (the what?) and pedagogy (the how?) of teaching, but how the curriculum is taught will be decided within each partnership in terms of the distribution between school- and university-based colleagues, and the distribution between theory sessions and school practice. This is one aspect of the pedagogy of teacher education, which is often shared with other professional courses which integrate academic input with workplace practice. One of the challenges of partnership working is that the different stakeholders involved on the ground, and their institutions, may not necessarily share the same conceptualisation of what constitutes effective teacher preparation. Opportunities to design and develop the curriculum can help to bring partners closer together in their understanding and direction of travel. Sometimes, however, these opportunities highlight irreconcilable differences, and institutions will choose to find a partnership to which they are more closely aligned in values and vision.

A further aspect of our pedagogy as teacher educators is that while teaching students, we are also modelling good practice. When this is made explicit, the students can critically reflect on the suitability of different pedagogical approaches for their own teaching (White, 2011). This means that students need opportunities alongside their experiences of explicit modelling so that they can explore different pedagogies in their own context. Leaving this to serendipity delays the progress of the student in developing their practice, so learning opportunities need to be carefully planned, carried out and evaluated by the student, with appropriate levels of support from expert colleagues. A collaborative approach to planning embraces the rich context in which the student and their mentor are working and will enable meaningful and effective professional learning for all involved.

Teacher education needs to equip teachers with the essential skill of research literacy so they can contribute to school curriculum development and develop research-informed practice. This means that teacher educators need to include critical engagement with learning theory and cutting-edge research to be able to lead and enact research-informed practice and for the evaluation of classroom practice (Boyd and White, 2017).

Assessing students

Many of us find that making authentic, appropriate and informed assessment decisions about the practice of students is a source of anxiety. It is often made more complex by those who are assessing having dual roles as a mentor and assessor, which they may experience as a conflict of interests (Tillema et al, 2011; Aspden and McLachlan, 2017). Having appropriate expectations of students for the stage of their training is challenging for new teacher educators, and needs to be revisited regularly by those with experience, in order to ensure judgements are consistent throughout a partnership and also across partnerships. There is more about quality assurance in Chapter 5. Stories of dilemmas experienced in assessing the teaching of students can form a helpful trigger for conversations within partnerships, to explore ways to frame those difficult conversations that need to take place to provoke personal development and improvements in practice.

CRITICAL **QUESTIONS**

Difficult conversations

No one likes having a confrontational conversation but if we value our students, colleagues or employees, we need to make time to talk honestly, rationally and clearly if there is a problem that needs dealing with. Having a plan will help. While dealing with a difficult issue, we are also modelling a process that shows respect for all, so we need to be professional and keep control of our emotions.

» When?

Having the conversation sooner rather than later will avoid extending any anxiety you have. Consider what will be happening for both of you after the conversation. It isn't helpful to have a difficult conversation last thing on Friday, or immediately before teaching a challenging class.

Allow enough time for the person to digest what is being said and to reflect. Make sure they have opportunity to express themselves.

» Where?

Finding a private and professional location is important.

» What will you say?

It is important to stick to the facts. Describe carefully the behaviour that has triggered the conversation. Describe the impact of the behaviour on others, for example, students, colleagues or yourself. Ensure the person understands why a change is needed.

Have the Teachers' Standards (DfE, 2012) and your own school/partnership policies to hand. If you need to draw attention to something within them, give the person time to read and reflect before responding. (Usually this level of detail is not needed.)

» Where should your focus be?

You must show respect for the individual as a person, focusing on their behaviour and not the individual.

You need to focus too on the solution, the way forward – what will the future look like? Are there specific procedures to put in place, or is a verbal commitment needed?

» What about afterwards?

Reflect on how you could have done better, and then move on. Think about how you can affirm the person when you next see them.

GUIDING AND ASSESSING STUDENTS

 TEACHER EDUCATOR **STORY 2.1**

Read through this story and see what teacher educator dilemma(s) you can spot.

In my role of school-based teacher educator (SBTE), supervising the training of students within my school, I monitor their progress. When I saw this third-year student for the first time working as a teacher in the group, my image was immediately very positive. She had a cheerful appearance, she was very positive towards the children and was open to feedback from her mentor and myself. The feedback she received was almost instantly visible in her lessons and actions. However, after the first 'personal development plan' and reflections, a number of points of attention emerged: not only were there many language errors, it lacked vision ... Why do you do what you do? On what do you base your choices? What considerations do you include in making your choice? In short, she had to go more in depth in her reflections and personal development plans. With this feedback the student started to work bravely and determinedly. In the days after this feedback conversation, we saw some development in the reflections and that feels good as a coach because it means you can make a difference for the student; you can take her to a higher level.

However, after a number of weeks the mentor wanted to talk to me about this student: the student followed up the feedback but the improvement was only of short duration. The feedback was used that week; however, it was not taken into the following week. Thus, the mentor had the feeling she had to start every week from scratch with the student; it wasn't a cumulative development. When I visited the student again in class, I also observed the points mentioned by the mentor. The pupils were less engaged at times, which requires appropriate action as a teacher, to act according to the pedagogical and educational needs of the pupils. After the lesson, we talked about this. It turned out that the student noticed the low level of involvement and unrest but didn't have sufficient personal resources to adequately respond to this. This is gained by experience, exercising, trying and reflecting. In consultation, we discussed extending the school-based training and a number of clear points were drawn up for attention. The student formulated higher and concrete objectives from these points.

The dilemma we faced, however, was that after a number of weeks the development we saw in this student wasn't sufficient; the student didn't react adequately to pupils' behaviour and needs. The question arose, when are we actually going to give an 'inadequate'? This student works very hard, but the development isn't the progress we would expect, considering that the guidance of her mentor was quite intensive. There were almost daily long reflective conversations and intensive coaching. With this student it was especially difficult because we very much hoped that she would succeed, because she worked hard, enjoyed working with the children and really wanted to grow and learn. That makes it incredibly difficult to remain objective and to focus on skills and competencies/ability.

> *For the mentor it's also difficult because a bond has been built up and it almost feels as if their guidance has been insufficient.*
>
> *What to do? We carefully considered the above issues. Discussions took place between mentor, student and institute-based teacher educator and we decided to consider the student's performance during previous school placements. We learnt that they showed the same pattern: a very energetic start, then a dip and by the end another sprint. In this way, the student was successful in her placement last year with the benefit of the doubt. All these cases have made us decide to assess her teaching as inadequate.*
>
> *It has really felt like a dilemma because you need to stay objective and at the same time give someone a positive experience. The golden question that supported our decision is 'Could we see this student run the class independently in half a year? Does she have sufficient skills to do this in a good way?'*
>
> *We look back on a constructive process in which we think we've acted carefully, by having a lot of coaching and giving timely feedback. It remains a shame to have to give an inadequate. However, all considerations and taking as many aspects as possible into account led us to the point where it eventually felt like a well-founded decision.*

CRITICAL **QUESTIONS**

Resonance/dissonance

- » What is your initial response?
- » How does this story relate to you and your practice as a teacher educator?
- » Which parts of the story resonate with you?
- » Which parts of the story conflict with your experience?
- » What difficult assessment decisions have you had to make?
- » Are there strategies that these teacher educators use that you would use?
- » Are there other strategies that you use that you would recommend in challenging assessment situations?

When a student is not making adequate progress, it is one thing to draw up clear points for attention; it is another to enable them to achieve those targets. How do you move from telling a student what they are not doing to scaffolding their learning and supporting development of appropriate skills?

GUIDING AND ASSESSING STUDENTS

 TEACHER EDUCATOR **STORY 2.2**

Read through Part 1 of this story.

PART 1: THE DILEMMA

During the professional task on inclusive education in school, the student examines the school's vision. They then collect pupil data from the school data management system; based on this, they visualise the educational needs of each child in a group. Using this complete group overview, the student will draw up and carry out a group plan for teaching a lesson. For this, the student may use existing group plans made by the classroom teacher. The assessment task for the programme consists of a presentation in which the student justifies how they organise and conduct inclusive education.

A dilemma for me, as the institute-based teacher educator (IBTE), is that not every school provides optimal learning opportunities for students to work on this task. The student therefore can't perform all professional activities properly. The biggest problem occurs during the collection of the pupil data. Not every mentor wants to give the student access to the pupil tracking system. The student can't meet the requirements set by the university for the group overview and the group plan. The gap between the university curriculum and the access and support provided by the workplace is too big. This dilemma occurred several times last school year and this school year.

CRITICAL **QUESTIONS**

Advice

» What would you advise the IBTE to do?

Now read through Part 2 of the story. Compare your plan of action to what happened.

» What are the similarities?
» What are the differences?

> **PART 2: THE SOLUTION**
>
> *From my role as co-ordinator of the professional task, I initially chose to inform the schools better during the preparatory meeting and in the periodic mailing. In the training for mentors, there was also specific attention given to guiding/coaching a student in working on the professional assignment. In my role, I've also raised this dilemma during the regular consultation with the school-based teacher educators (SBTEs) in this group of schools. The SBTE must ensure that the student gets all the necessary learning opportunities in the workplace/school. And last, but not least, I informed the IBTE who visits the students in the schools. After all, they are the link between the university and the school.*
>
> *The better provision of information has led to the problem occurring less often. Nevertheless, there was still one school during this period that didn't allow two students to access the necessary data. I advised these students to contact the IBTE, who immediately checked with the SBTE and mentors about how the student can still access the required data. They have pointed out that the data are being used by the students with care and are being anonymised. Ultimately, in this specific case, the choice was made to give the student limited access to the pupil monitoring system and the test results. This means that the students have to work at the school on the group overview and the group plans, so that the data stays within the school.*

CRITICAL QUESTIONS

Affordance

The affordance (or invitational quality) of the school is facilitated through seeing students as colleagues, opening up all teaching activities for students and having a clear policy for initial teacher education.

Four types of activities are available for students at school:

- activities with or for pupils, eg planning, teaching and assessment;
- activities at school level, eg communicating with parents, colleagues and other professionals;
- accessibility and use of school-based resources, eg pupil files, school data, intranet and staff library;
- activities aimed at teacher professional development, eg staff professional learning opportunities and feedback talks with the mentor.

The affordance of partner schools may be based on the individual decisions of mentors instead of on shared views regarding the training of students. Individual mentors, even

GUIDING AND ASSESSING STUDENTS

within schools, can differ considerably in which activities they expect from students, which activities they allow them to do and which activities are not available (van Velzen and Timmermans, 2014).

» In what ways do you ensure that activities that are provided in school are related to the learning needs of the individual students?

TEACHER EDUCATOR **STORY 2.3**

Read through this story and see what teacher educator dilemma(s) you can spot.

Rosalind was a graduate from a top university, black, and from a working-class background. After graduating, Rosalind worked for several years as a policy advisor for a government department before deciding to train as a secondary teacher. Her main school-based experience was at a neighbouring school between September and April after which her second school-based experience was in my school where I was head of department and SBTE, having oversight for students. Rosalind had started her course well, passing the first end of term assessment with no major concerns or issues, but she had not met the standards for the second end of term assessment. It was agreed that her IBTE and I would reassess her after two weeks in her second school. In not meeting the standards for this assessment, Rosalind's first school mentor felt that she lacked confidence and presence in the class, her lessons did not have a clear learning objective or focus and her lesson activities did not engage pupils sufficiently and were not differentiated. It was perceived that the difficulties faced by Rosalind in her first school were complicated by her becoming pregnant during the period of school-based experience, with some absences in the early stages of her pregnancy. She was due to give birth in the August.

On first meeting Rosalind, I was struck by the contrast between my first impressions of her and the reasons given for her not meeting the standards. To me, Rosalind appeared to be a quietly confident, warm, funny and open person. One of the requirements of students for their second school experience was for them to 'go in cold' with at least one class by teaching the pupils the very first time they meet them. The rationale for this was to prepare each student for the beginning of their year as a newly qualified teacher in September when they would be expected to teach a number of different classes on first meeting. It was planned for Rosalind to 'go in cold' with one of my mixed ability Year 8 classes, who could be challenging – chatty and with some low-level disruption. The lesson was very successful. Rosalind was a calm and confident presence in the classroom, effectively dealing with unwanted behaviour. The lesson was clearly focused and learning activities engaged all pupils and helped them make progress. Yes, there were areas that needed

> *to be developed and improved, for example, stretch and challenge for the more able, but to me it was clear that Rosalind could teach. During the feedback afterwards, Rosalind started by focusing on what had gone wrong in the lesson, and I prompted her several times to focus on the positives and what had gone well. Once Rosalind had recognised what had gone well in the lesson, and importantly why, she appeared to relax, and we could constructively discuss what she could do differently next time. From this initial lesson and feedback, Rosalind went from strength to strength in her practice, comfortably passing her reassessment and successfully completing her final assessment and the course. She was always too discreet and professional to go into detail, but I was aware from her university tutor that there had been difficulties in her relationship with her first school mentor, particularly once she said she was pregnant. In August, Rosalind had a healthy baby boy, and returned to teaching to start her year as a newly qualified teacher outside of the area.*
>
> *Looking back, the key factors which enabled Rosalind to successfully complete her teacher training were:*
>
> » *a willingness to take a student [or any colleague for that matter] at face value and not to pre-judge on what had happened elsewhere;*
>
> » *the importance of emphasising the positives in a student's practice during feedback;*
>
> » *providing students with the space to critically reflect in a positive and supportive manner;*
>
> » *the opportunity for a student to start afresh if a period of school-based training does not work out.*

CRITICAL **QUESTIONS**

Dealing with challenges

Read the story and consider what the challenge is.

» In what way do you identify with this incident? Have you experienced anything similar?

» What would you do in this situation? What choices would you make? Discuss together.

» Reflect on your learning from this story. Is there something that you can take with you to develop your own practice, or the practice in your partnership?

COACHING **QUESTIONS**

> How do you deal with making difficult decisions which will impact on students/colleagues who you have developed a close relationship with?
> (Story 2.1)

> Where are the spaces that enable you to build understanding of expectations and contexts between partners?
> How could you use these opportunities more effectively?
> (Story 2.2)

> How do you help each other to appreciate some of our deeply held assumptions?
> How can you develop the environment in which you are working to surface issues of unconscious bias that need addressing?
> (Story 2.3)

REFLECTIONS

Some of the challenges around assessment that we experience as teacher educators are around the quality of the guidance and learning opportunities that have been provided to the student during their training. There is a danger of 'judgementoring' (Hobson, 2016), where instead of the mentor being a supporter alongside the student in their professional learning journey, the mentor–student relationship is damaged by the frequency of the mentor's evaluations of the student's planning and teaching. We need to learn how to scaffold our students' learning and development, explaining how to carry out different aspects of practice rather than telling them what they are not doing.

Where difficult conversations are needed, it is important to provide support to new teacher educators in the partnership who may not have experience in carrying out difficult conversations with colleagues and students. It is an essential skill to develop; providing shadowing and mentoring to explain professional decisions can be effective ways to develop teacher educator practice across the partnership.

The second principle for initial teacher education partnerships that Mutton et al (2018) propose is the need for a curriculum that enables students to get the most from their school-based experiences. When a curriculum is designed and developed by involving the strengths of different stakeholders in the partnership, learning opportunities can be created that are appropriate to the context and student needs.

Guiding and assessing students must be appropriate to the current context, so there needs to be flexibility and agility within partnerships to respond to changing situations, whether due to policy changes or environmental issues. Such adaptations will include curriculum content and pedagogical approaches that students will need to develop for their teaching context. Partnerships that have a strong shared vision for the sort of teachers that they are preparing, and strong beliefs about their core purposes and values, will be more resilient in times of change (Gu and Day, 2013).

Further resources

Loughran, J (2006) *Developing a Pedagogy of Teacher Education: Understanding Teaching and Learning about Teaching.* London: Routledge.

This book explores the complex nature of teaching and of learning about teaching, illustrating how important teacher educators' professional knowledge is and how that knowledge must influence teacher training practices. It highlights the layered nature of learning to teach – concentrating not only on the content of the curriculum, but also on the way that teacher educators teach about teaching.

O'Leary, M (2020) *Classroom Observation.* 2nd ed. London: Routledge.

This practical book explores the role of lesson observation in teacher development. It includes a critical analysis of the use of lesson observation for professional learning and assessment.

Russell, T and Loughran, J (eds) (2007) *Enacting a Pedagogy of Teacher Education: Values, Relationships and Practice.* Abingdon: Routledge.

This book contains a collection of articles, written by practitioners, on how individuals enact pedagogy in the context of teacher education. It is founded on the belief that when teacher educators are teaching and demonstrating how to teach simultaneously, the quality of teacher education improves.

References

Aspden, K M and McLachlan, C (2017) A Complex Act—Teacher Educators Share Their Perspectives of Practicum Assessment. *Waikato Journal of Education*, 22(3): 21–32.

Boyd, P and White, E (2017) Teacher Educator Professional Inquiry in an Age of Accountability. In Boyd, P and Szplit, A (eds) *Teachers and Teacher Educators Learning Through Inquiry: International Perspectives.* Kraków: Attyka. [online] Available at: http://researchprofiles.herts.ac.uk/portal/files/12126690/Teacher_Educator_Professional_Inquiry_in_an_Age_of_Accountability._Boyd_White_2017.pdf (accessed 6 February 2021).

Department for Education (DfE) (2012) *Teachers' Standards.* [online] Available at: www.gov.uk/government/publications/teachers-standards (accessed 6 February 2021).

Department for Education (DfE) (2019) *ITT Core Content Framework*. [online] Available at: www.gov.uk/government/publications/initial-teacher-training-itt-core-content-framework (accessed 6 February 2021).

Gu, Q and Day, C (2013) Challenges to Teacher Resilience: Conditions Count. *British Educational Research Journal*, 39: 22–44.

Hobson, A J (2016) Judgementoring and How to Avert It: Introducing ONSIDE Mentoring for Beginning Teachers. *International Journal of Mentoring and Coaching in Education*, 5: 87–110.

Mutton, T, Burn, K, Hagger, H and Thirlwell, K (2018) *Teacher Education Partnerships: Policy and Practice*. St Albans: Critical Publishing.

Tillema, H H, Smith, K and Leshem, S (2011) Dual Roles – Conflicting Purposes: A Comparative Study on Perceptions on Assessment in Mentoring Relations During Practicum. *European Journal of Teacher Education*, 34(2): 139–59.

van Velzen, C V and Timmermans, M (2014) What Can We Learn from the Shift Towards a More School-centred Model in the Netherlands? In Jones, K and White, E (eds) *Developing Outstanding School-Based Teacher Education*. St Albans: Critical Publishing.

White, E (2011) Working Towards Explicit Modelling: Experiences of a New Teacher Educator. *Professional Development in Education*, 37: 483–97.

CHAPTER 3 | WORKING COLLABORATIVELY

KEY **THEMES**

This chapter is about:
- *communication in partnerships;*
- *roles of teacher educators in the partnership;*
- *working in partnership within an institution;*
- *working in partnership across institutions.*

TEACHER EDUCATOR **STORIES**

Teacher educator story 3.1 is written by an institute-based teacher educator about working collaboratively with school-based teacher educators.

Teacher educator story 3.2 is written by a school-based teacher educator about the communication between the initial teacher education provider and the school.

Teacher educator story 3.3 is written by a school-based teacher educator about working with colleagues to promote learning from school-based practice.

Tensions within teacher education partnerships

Partnerships in initial teacher education may have inherent tensions due to the differing priorities of schools on educating their pupils and universities on educating students. The differing conceptions of how teachers should be prepared (the balance between academic and workplace learning) and differing views of the goal of teacher preparation (a teacher for our school now, or a professional prepared for a changing educational landscape) can also be sources of tension. Working to overcome these tensions is an ongoing process of bringing together stakeholders from all institutions involved in the partnership, and developing the quality of communication, co-operation and collaboration. These important relationships can be challenging to maintain with turnover of teacher educators in schools and universities as careers develop and responsibilities change.

In order to improve the collaboration within our partnerships, it is important that we develop a shared vision for the kind of teachers that we are preparing; a curriculum where responsibilities are clearly delineated, working to the strengths of the partners and their unique settings; and a clear understanding of the roles of respective participants in the partnership. Bringing partners together to a shared vision when conceptions differ is complex. It is important to have a 'third space' where conversations can go deeper than setting up shared procedures (Zeichner, 2010).

Using stories of challenges in practice can provide a stimulation to develop our understanding of our current professional practices, learning from the perspectives of the different stakeholders. Our partnership work is multi-levelled, drawing in those in the classroom, staff room, school, School of Education office at the university and management and beyond. In-depth consideration of incidents that are experienced as dilemmas by the storytellers can help us appreciate the complexity of our partnerships, and identify who needs to be engaged in making improvements in our practice on the ground and in developing our core partnership vision and values.

TEACHER EDUCATOR **STORY 3.1**

Read through this story and see what teacher educator dilemma(s) you can spot.

For many years I worked as a teacher in secondary education and as a school-based teacher educator (SBTE) overseeing the placement of students in my school. Four years ago I started to work as an institute-based teacher educator (IBTE).

Sometime around mid-October I went to the first meeting of the team with SBTEs of different teaching schools with whom I work as an IBTE. This SBTE team had already had several meetings this academic year. Only recently I received the invitation to attend this meeting. I notice that I'm somewhat nervous. The reason is that I know that this SBTE team has had an unpleasant experience with an IBTE colleague of mine who attended the meetings in the past. The SBTEs would rather train the students alone, without the co-operation of an IBTE colleague from the university. But that isn't what the partnership is about, so an IBTE must join with the SBTE team. That IBTE is me! My assignment – especially directed by my university – is to join and to NOT be the all- or better-knowing IBTE; OK – that's the role I must play. I'm a little nervous, and ask myself: will I be accepted by them?

After the introductions (who is who, and the goal of the meeting), I receive the material that's going to be used by the students in the upcoming weeks. Just to get insight into the process of how this material is developed, I ask for the minutes of the last meetings. It turned out there are none, but they seem to like the idea to make notes during every meeting and add it to a list of agreements made. So, would they live up to expectations? I'm feeling a little bit awkward and am thinking 'I hope they don't think that I think that they aren't professional'.

While they were talking about several things that were nothing to do with me I browse the material the SBTE team made for the students. Coincidently, the references got my attention because they didn't conform to referencing that we require the students to use;

this referencing system should also be used correctly in teaching materials for students, developed by SBTEs. Realising that I'm instructed not to be the wise IBTE, I hesitate to mention it. I am waiting for the right moment, so I'm glad that one of the SBTEs brings up some minor things that should be changed. During tea break I tell the SBTEs 'While you have to make some changes as asked, perhaps you could also take a look at the references. A couple of books aren't referred to properly, using the referencing system. I just noticed'. One of the SBTEs says thanks. It seems OK.

After the break we discuss the material, especially the themes and content concerning the first meeting for the students at their schools. Listening to what is said, I realise that they don't consider the authentic context of the school as a valuable input to learn from. That is a pity; that is one of the main reasons for workplace learning. What to do? How to act? Gosh…! I decide to tell them how I as an IBTE work with students at the institute when these themes are on the timetable and how jealous I am of the SBTEs because they have their own authentic and rich environment (that is also the environment of the student) to refer to while discussing the themes. One of the SBTEs gets the point and reacts: 'We could ask the students to do some observations and afterwards we can discuss what they saw with them and their mentors'. All of a sudden the SBTEs have a lot of interesting new ideas about connecting the themes to the context and the learning opportunities that the school can provide. They write them down. Their enthusiasm does take me along… The meeting ends. The SBTEs thank me. I am invited to come again. Phew!

CRITICAL **QUESTIONS**

Perspective taking

» Who are the participants in the story?

» Look at the story from their perspectives. What does each person have to gain or lose?

Good communication is required for working at a basic cooperative level… Cooperation occurs between partners who are working as free agents and choosing to work towards a common goal… [Collaboration] is not only working towards a shared outcome but having a shared process to get there.

(White and Dickerson, 2016, p 65)

Collaboration is a complex, sophisticated process. It requires competence, confidence and commitment on the part of all parties involved. Respect and trust, both for oneself and others, is key to collaboration. As such, patience, nurturance and time are required to build a relationship to the point where collaboration can occur.

(Henneman et al, 1995, p 108)

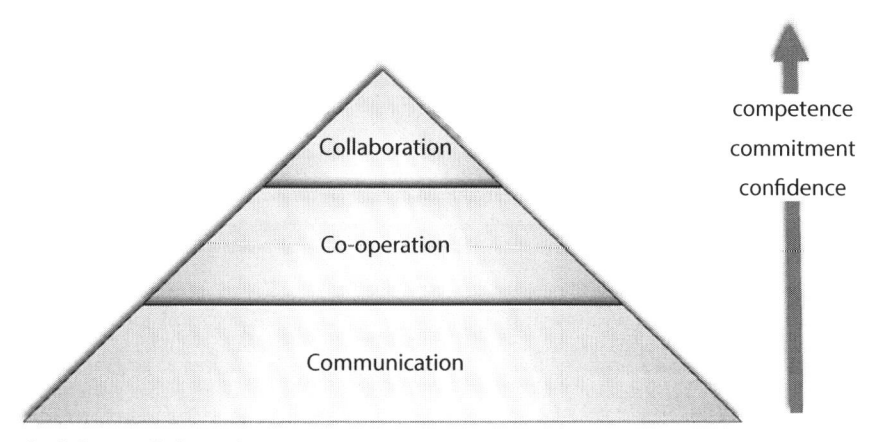

Figure 3.1 Building collaboration

CRITICAL **QUESTIONS**

Collaborating

Consider the quotations above and Figure 3.1.

» To what extent are the teacher educators gaining in confidence, commitment and competence in this story?

» How is this reflected in the move from communicating to co-operating and then deeper collaboration together of these individuals?

TEACHER EDUCATOR **STORY 3.2**

Read through this story and see what teacher educator dilemma(s) you can spot.

This year, together with a colleague from the university, I was responsible for the support meetings for a group of students from a cluster of schools. I am also the school-based teacher educator (SBTE) for a number of these students.

A colleague of mine is the teacher mentor of one of these students, Julia. During the placement, I receive signals from my colleague that Julia has many targets. During the support meetings this doesn't really come up with Julia. I notice that she misses the support meetings a number of times. When I ask her personally after a meeting how she's getting on with the placement, she is short and says only 'It's going well'. She then rushes away. At a later moment I try to speak to her again but now separately and Julia indicates that there are private problems at the workplace that she'll discuss with me.

A week later, I hear that Julia has had an observation visit from the institute-based teacher educator (IBTE) and that the teacher mentor and IBTE came to the conclusion that Julia will have to extend her placement to work on her targets. The first session after this, Julia isn't at the support meeting and a week later I receive the announcement from her teacher mentor, my colleague, that Julia has stopped the placement. Julia hasn't contacted me about this; not in my role in facilitating the support meetings nor in my role as SBTE. After a conversation with my colleague, Julia's teacher mentor, I plan to contact Julia's IBTE and arrange an appointment. Due to other work priorities, I didn't make it. It's now two months later and the IBTE has contacted our school and I want to arrange a conversation with the IBTE and Julia.

My dilemma has several aspects for me. The first aspect is my double role: SBTE and facilitator of the support group. During the support meetings, I want to pay attention to all students but a number of students want more of my attention. At those meetings I try to talk with the students that I also deal with as an SBTE. However, I notice that I don't get any contact with them in those meetings.

The second aspect has to do with the question 'Who is responsible for the student's learning?' I would like to know what's going on, but I also feel that I should keep my distance because the student is responsible for their own learning. When I push the door a bit and the student shuts the door, what should I do? I have chosen to focus mainly on contact via the teacher mentor.

The third aspect has to do with communication between the university and school. Am I the one who needs to contact the IBTE? At first, I thought so. Now that I've not done it due to lack of time, and the IBTE contacted me, I think that's fine too. As an SBTE, I inform the teacher mentors about the students. This raises the question 'Who is responsible for the contact between the IBTE and the training school?'

I experience the co-operation between the university and workplace as far as the support meetings are concerned as very pleasant and valuable. Students also point out that they experience this as added value. I find the co-operation at workplace level between the university and school (SBTEs/mentors) more difficult.

CRITICAL **QUESTIONS**

Role playing

» Read the story. Put yourself into the shoes of each of the participants in the story, one at a time. Describe the challenge from their perspective. What alternative endings would they give the story?

» How would you deal with each aspect that the SBTE is experiencing as a dilemma?

TEACHER EDUCATOR **STORY 3.3**

Read through this story and see what teacher educator dilemma(s) you can spot.

It's November and my head is in my hands... what should I do with my final-year student group? Fourteen hardworking students, who do, do, do, do, do, without learning.

We are a training school and as a school-based teacher educator (SBTE), I have many years of experience with the final-year students, developed in collaboration with the university. These students learn and have a small job/salary with us. They do their entire programme in practice: research, peer review, portfolio guidance, and training on diverse research themes. Usually, I have the whole group after their three weeks in the 'learning mode' and the students experience this as liberation: 'Oh, it isn't about the rules and the models that I use, but about focusing on pupil learning and therefore becoming a good teacher? Wow!' I have got used to this reaction. But this group is different! They are task-oriented, linking everything to the standards as quickly as possible, and quickly completing everything. They find the progress interviews a revelation 'What good questions do you ask? Why is this useful?' But everything we do in the group leads to sighing, disinterest, and even rebellion. The students are sometimes dismissive of the expert teachers who provide workshops, and there are reproaches such as 'this wasn't communicated well'; nobody seems to be open. What now?

This year, for the first time, I don't have control over the trajectory of the programme on my own. I coach/guide/teach the group with three colleagues from my school and the university. We thought that would be fine: we are now working with learning outcomes instead of with prescribed formats. Each student has to formulate how he or she will show that they've achieved certain goals. Ideal, right? How is it possible that it doesn't work? The students all seem to want to find something secure to hold on to and no one is really experimenting... I'm talking to my colleagues. What's happening? What must we do? One of them says: 'It will come naturally; they need more time'. But I see that this is going to take too long. I can't go on like this. I find it difficult because we're working together. I would prefer to find out how we're going to solve it. However, I've also seen that, in theory, we're on the same page as colleagues, but not in the implementation. What now? I decide to do an intervention. Just try it!

I'm going to talk to the group on my own. I let them tell me extensively about their frustrations. I keep my mouth shut... oh, how difficult... because there's so much on the table that I would like to respond with 'yes', but...'. I only ask questions: ask for clarification, explanation and reactions from others in the group. The group is relieved. 'We feel that we've really been listened to now.' There are early signs that not everything is bad; there are also good things. They feel a heavy burden and are afraid they won't succeed. I answer: 'So you're using this year, which has been specially designed, not to learn as much as possible, because you think you can do that easily afterwards?' A conversation about expectations arises. If you learn all year, I promise you will succeed. That's just what is going to happen. For the first time I have the idea that they will trust me. Step 1, I think.

I took another step a week or two later. I have talked about learning, choosing terms that the students can't connect directly to their familiar repertoire. I speak about three-dimensional learning (instead of about cyclic learning), and I contextualise it, including about learning from failures. Something is bubbling. Another week later I ask: 'Which teacher of Harry Potter is a good teacher and why?' A lively discussion arises. But I also do something else. I have a consultation with my colleagues. We share our perceptions and we explore what they mean. We talk about how we've experienced the first weeks, including where it relates to each other's actions. What did we do that meant the students weren't in learning mode? That provided many insights. I'm only now completely honest about what I thought about the start, what I saw and what I did myself. I realise that I should have done this much sooner. We make plans for the next year (to start differently) and we discuss how we'll continue to deal with this group.

In mid-January I notice the result. The group is in a different position with respect to learning. Success! There is a different attitude, there is more adventure, there is more confidence. There is learning. What a relief. I myself have also learnt. I'd rather connect with colleagues, take more account of what I see and feel with the students and engage with them earlier.

CRITICAL **QUESTIONS**

What's it all about? – group activity

» Give the story a title. Compare the title you chose with that of others in your pair or triplet.
» Discuss the story. What do you think are the key issues that it highlights? You may find different issues from each other.
» Why were you drawn to the issue you identified?
» Do you want to change the story title you chose?
» Look at the key issues you have identified in your group. Are they about the SBTE, the students, the programme…?
» Explore one of the issues in more depth. In what ways can we:
   a) prepare students for their school-based experience and manage their expectations?
   b) help students to focus on their professional learning, rather than ticking boxes?
   c) support colleagues to develop an understanding of how to promote workplace learning?
   d) support colleagues in developing the necessary competences of SBTEs?

COACHING **QUESTIONS**

What strategies can you employ to clarify roles and responsibilities where there are grey areas? (Story 3.2)

How can you help your mentors to use the full potential of their workplace for student learning (Story 3.1)

Is this student focused on meeting the standards and getting qualified rather than focused on their professional learning? Are there ways that you can help the focus to shift? How can you lead the dialogue and/or the learning opportunities towards a different focus? (Story 3.3)

> **REFLECTIONS**
>
> Initial teacher education partnerships are often established between institutions at the level of the leadership and management, while those working 'on the ground' have to create realistic working practices. This requires commitment to communication; establishment of clear roles and responsibilities; and providing a third space where stakeholders can explore the perspectives that each hold, from their different contexts and experiences. The advantage is that *'third spaces involve a rejection of binaries such as practitioner and academic knowledge and theory and practice and involve the integration of what are often seen as competing discourses in new ways—an either/or perspective is transformed into a both/also point of view'* (Zeichner, 2010, p 92). Collaboration requires the building of trusting relationships, which takes time and needs to be specifically planned for. This is important between teacher educators both within an institution, and between institutions who are working in partnership, so is something that the leadership and management in each institution in the partnership need to plan for.
>
> It can be easy to focus on structures, processes and procedures when meeting together across the partnership, but although these form an important foundation, they can draw our attention away from quality dialogue focused on the learning of pupils and of professionals.

Further resource

Mutton, T, Burn, K, Hagger, H and Thirlwell, K (2018) *Teacher Education Partnerships: Policy and Practice*. St Albans: Critical Publishing.

This book surveys and critiques partnership developments in recent years in England, analyses a case study of a school-centred initial teacher training provider and provides a set of helpful principles to underpin effective partnership working.

References

Henneman, E A, Lee, J L and Cohen, J I (1995) Collaboration: A Concept Analysis. *Journal of Advanced Nursing*, 21: 103–9.

White, E and Dickerson, C (2016) Supporting the Re-balancing of Initial Teacher Education within University and School Partnerships. *Journal of the World Federation of Associations of Teacher Education*, 1(2): 64–76. [online] Available at: www.worldfate.org/docpdf/journal_01-02.pdf (accessed 6 February 2021).

Zeichner, K (2010) Rethinking the Connections between Campus Courses and Field Experiences in College- and University-based Teacher Education. *Journal of Teacher Education*, 61(1–2): 89–99.

CHAPTER 4 | PROFESSIONALISM AND WELL-BEING

KEY **THEMES**

This chapter is about:
- *the professionalism of teacher educators;*
- *the professionalism of students;*
- *the well-being of students.*

TEACHER EDUCATOR **STORIES**

Teacher educator story 4.1 is written by an institute-based teacher educator about a challenge that arose during a student's assessment.

Teacher educator story 4.2 is written by an institute-based teacher educator about a safeguarding issue.

Teacher educator story 4.3 is written by a school-based teacher educator about working with a student who has a mental health issue.

Developing personally and professionally

Identity is how we portray ourselves to others and the way we make sense of who we are. It is embedded in our culture. Our identities as teachers and teacher educators go beyond our role. They develop in dynamic interaction with others in our professional context. Through this interaction, we learn the roles of others in relation to ourselves and how to behave towards others and our work environment (Beijaard et al, 2004). Day and Kington (2008) propose three interacting dimensions of teacher identity: professional; situated; and personal. There are often tensions between the professional, personal, emotional and social elements of teachers' experiences, which impact on their sense of identity. These dimensions can be extrapolated for teacher educators too, while remembering that a teacher identity is different from a teacher educator identity.

Professional identity

This reflects social and policy expectations of what a good teacher/teacher educator is and the educational ideals of the teacher/teacher educator. Our professional identity affects our *'sense of purpose, self-efficacy, motivation, commitment, job satisfaction and effectiveness'* (Day et al, 2006, p 601).

Situated identity

Our immediate work setting helps to form our identity. This dimension is affected by conditions locally and by feedback received from colleagues and pupils/students. Lave and Wenger (1991) refer to this as situated learning in a community of practice, which newcomers have access to through legitimate participation on the periphery of the community.

Personal identity

This dimension is located outside the educational setting, linked to family, friends and other external and internal influences that impact on who we are.

Teachers and teacher educators hold implicit beliefs about their role and responsibilities. Reflective practices help us to consciously direct our development at different stages of our careers through surfacing our implicit beliefs and opening them up for interrogation. Using stories of challenges in practice can help us to explore the causes of some of the tensions we experience between the professional, personal and situated dimensions of our identity. When we entered the profession we may have considered the kind of teacher/teacher educator we would like to become. Further examination individually, or in collaboration with colleagues and partners, can enable us to adapt and grow personally and professionally. Constant change is a part of professional life, and flexibility, agility and an open mind are valuable traits to develop. Unless we are prepared to do this identity work for ourselves, we are not well-placed to be able to support those entering the profession.

As teacher educators we have an influence on the identity of the teachers we are working with. We may experience many incidents and have opportunities to lead the professional development of our students in a very specific and personal way. Being able to identify these incidents in the moment and to step back and see the bigger picture and consider what can be learnt through it are an important part of our own professional learning. A helpful approach can be – what additional learning is there in this incident that will help this student to develop a professional attitude? For example, a student who causes friction with other colleagues may have a problem in school that can be sorted out simply on the ground. If we limit our intervention to sorting out the problem for the student, we will have missed the opportunity for this student to consider professional ways of raising issues that are causing them discomfort.

Sometimes our student(s) observe us having to deal with issues arising in the moment, in a professional way. This can be a great learning opportunity, to be explicit about how we dealt with an issue and to open it up for discussion with the student(s).

Developing resilience

Being resilient is being able to respond innovatively to a changing educational landscape. Sometimes we hear people blaming others for their lack of resilience when, in fact, their expectations have been unreasonable. Having a resilient attitude can enable us to be agile and make wise and innovative responses to reasonable challenges, but also to be able to challenge others when they have unreasonable expectations of us.

We are experiencing a period of exponential change within our profession, due to huge changes occurring in the world around us. Many find change challenging, and it is important to be compassionate towards others who may be experiencing changes differently from ourselves. We need to also be appreciative of the impact that these changes can have on the well-being of students and the other stakeholders in initial teacher education. Encouraging and establishing different working patterns that maintain our mental health and physical safety requires careful consideration of local and national guidelines and drawing on research and resources to inform what might work in our partnerships. Research indicates that having strong beliefs about our core purposes and values, and having support from colleagues and leaders, or a combination of these are essential in contributing to the development of individual and collective resilience (Gu and Day, 2013). Firstly, looking at our beliefs: a good starting point in preparation for teacher education is to ask ourselves what the key messages are about our ethos and vision and how we can embed these effectively with the tools we have available, whether working online or within our settings. We may need to develop agility and be able to let go of the structures that have worked well in the past and been refined over many years. When we keep asking ourselves what the best way is to meet the purpose, it is easier to embrace change and to bring others with us. Secondly, considering our relationships, we must consider whether we are able to dedicate the time and attention we need to develop supportive relationships with partners across the boundaries between our educational establishments.

Teachers' feelings about their workload and their identities as excellent, committed professionals are complex. Going forward it is important that we learn to talk, think and act differently about workload, as the culture of extreme workload in pursuit of perpetual improvement is embedded in a whole generation of teachers. If workload is going to become professionally acceptable, then we (the workforce) must be central to our own reform. Without significant shifts in perceptions of 'work' by all members of school communities, nothing can change (Greer and Daly, 2019).

As we develop confident teachers with the agency to make professional judgements that enable the development and learning of all, and the professional voice to be able to articulate how research has informed their practice and contributed to new thinking and new ways of working, they will become more resilient and be able to respond innovatively to a changing educational landscape.

TEACHER EDUCATOR **STORY 4.1**

Read through this story and see what teacher educator dilemma(s) you can spot.

PART 1

I am an institute-based teacher educator (IBTE), with ten years of experience in secondary teacher education. When I parked my car on a beautiful day shortly before the summer holidays, at a big secondary school, I didn't know that something unexpected was going to happen that morning. The school-based teacher educator (SBTE) who was co-ordinating

> *the teacher training within the school, the mentors and I were planning to carry out final assessments of six students. We had prepared for the assessments thoroughly, having read through their school-based evidence, prepared questions and discussed possible marks. There was no reason for us to have concerns about the results. The mentors had given their advice on the feedback and mark the student should get, and I would verify the final assessment, because the university is ultimately accountable. Everything was complete; we would interview the students and determine the final marks. Then the placement would be over; and the students could concentrate on their academic exams and then enjoy the summer holidays.*
>
> *The conversations started around a small table with four chairs: one for the SBTE, one for the student, one for the mentor and one for me, the IBTE. The first conversations went as expected. I asked critical questions about the student's professional development around the school-based training competences. The students named their strengths, weaknesses and their learning targets for the new academic year. Personal attention was paid to the well-being of each student, successes were recognised, and reciprocal thanks expressed by students and the colleagues of the school. There were no special details about the sixth student, so I thought the assessments were almost finished. Now I realise that the challenge started at that moment!*
>
> *The mentor of the sixth student entered the room, with steam coming from his ears! The student joined us. The mentor was given the floor and he spoke the disquieting words: 'This student will not pass'. Everyone was shocked: what happened, what had changed? The first assessment seemed positive, and now this? The mentor explained that the student should have gone on a school trip the day before and had cancelled at the last minute. This unprofessional attitude of the student had led to a complicated organisational problem for the other supervisors of the group. What now?*

CRITICAL **QUESTIONS**

Before you read on…

» What would you advise the IBTE to do?

» Read the second part of the story and compare your solution with what happened.

Part 2

I knew immediately that this couldn't be a reason to give an inadequate assessment, as the student is only learning. The mentor was very angry, and actually he had a point. The student had tears in his eyes. The SBTE looked at me uncomfortably and let me have the floor. I straightened my back and immediately decided to address the student on his responsibility: 'Is this correct? Do you understand that this is very annoying for your colleagues; what happened?' The story was right: due to a delay in traffic, the student couldn't have got to school on time and he made the choice, while he was driving, to step down, while his colleagues and pupils were already waiting for him. And yes, he understood that it was very annoying for colleagues and he understood the anger of the mentor, but he had no idea how he could solve this now.

Honestly, me neither. Firstly, I wanted to get the atmosphere in the conversation back in the right direction as quickly as possible. I took the decision to proceed directly to the business of the assessment process, discussing the competences with the completed assessment form before us, until we were at the last standard, including teamwork. That gave some breathing space for people to calm down, I hoped. During the discussion of some of the earlier competences, something special happened. The student said that he was the football coach of a youth team. He considered his classes as his team, in which each pupil had his own role. He taught the pupils to accept each other's roles and to work together for their learning. He didn't have problems with behaviour management, he was popular with pupils and colleagues, and his pupils had good results. He was very consistent in his practice. His vision was that he never wanted to exclude a pupil. He didn't do that in his football team either; every player is needed to achieve the best result. The integrity and the outspoken vision that permeated his story were disarming.

The SBTE nodded approvingly, and I saw a solution. Everyone would benefit from a quick conclusion of the conversation. I briefly summarised the issues: the unexpected and unwelcome behaviour of the student; his successes; his vision; and the irritation that he'd caused to his colleagues. I proposed, in my role as IBTE and moderator, that during the period until the summer holidays the student could participate twice more with colleagues at the school, to evidence working together with them for the competency. He would carry out a number of directed tasks in consultation with his mentor. As moderator, I would consider the recorded evidence following those activities and the conclusions of the current conversation and I would agree a final grade. Everyone took a sigh of relief and agreed. We shook hands and wished each other a good holiday. On the way to my car, the student caught up with me. The only thing he said was: 'Do you know how alone I felt yesterday?' He wiped his eyes, 'but I'm going to fix it, I'm going to work very hard these last days'. In the end, the placement was passed.

My challenge was to lead the assessment conversation professionally, to stand up for the student, and in the meantime not to let down the colleagues from the school and achieve a fair assessment grade. Unexpectedly, the input from the student gave me the opportunity

> to 'bend' the conversation. What I learnt was to always keep listening carefully, taking into account unexpected situations and, if necessary, vigorously take control in a conversation if it goes the wrong way. In addition, I've realised that an IBTE could be a coach of a team of students. Now I regularly discuss this idea in meetings with colleagues inside and outside the institute.

CRITICAL QUESTIONS

After reading Part 2 and comparing your solution with what happened…

» What are the similarities?
» What are the differences?
» Reflect on your learning from this story and the activity.

TEACHER EDUCATOR STORY 4.2

Read through this story and see what teacher educator dilemma(s) you can spot.

I am a secondary institute-based teacher educator (IBTE) with several years' experience. When I saw Michael, I wondered what had happened. He was tense and his eyes were downcast. Yes, he wanted to talk to me to see if I'd already heard what was going on at school... Visibly moved by what was happening, we looked for a place to talk.

The school-based teacher educator (SBTE) overseeing the students on placement in the school had previously emailed me. The message was that the school management and Michael's teacher mentor were in contact with the police; there was a hassle with some of the pupils. It was really important that I see Michael today. 'Well, it was quite something', I heard him say in a defeated voice. He carefully outlined the situation that had taken place two days ago. Coming into the staff room, he saw a colleague showing his mobile to another colleague. 'Look...' said this colleague. Michael saw a picture of himself in a flash and shouted amazed, 'Hey, that's me!' The colleagues included Michael, and together they looked at an Instagram account. Michael's picture was posted on a 'weird' account associated with some strange insinuations about paedophiles.

Michael looked at me with wide eyes: 'Who does things like this?' and then 'Why are they doing this to me?' He felt defeated and wanted no stone unturned: 'I want to know why they do this'. He asked me not to rest until his photo and the text on Instagram were removed. His mentor attempted to find out via social media to whom the account belonged and how the information could be removed. The police let us get on with it. Michael wanted nothing more than to tell the truth and for 'my photo with that nonsense removed from that account, as soon as possible'. 'Why do pupils do this? Why me?' With these pressing questions, Michael's resilience and tolerance were being tested.

Like Michael, I was also affected. What was the best way to guide him working with his colleagues? The school regularly works with students. I knew Michael's doubts about his career choice and saw that this event hit him deeply. He kept asking himself, 'Why me? What did I do?' He and his colleagues had a suspicion about where the insinuations had come from. The headteacher, in collaboration with the police, tried to speed up the investigation. Michael was involved in the investigation, but the three weeks in which the conversations took place were a rollercoaster for him. Together with his mentor, he decided which lessons he wanted to teach. I was informed regularly about developments and maintained contact with Michael's tutor and the school management.

He spoke openly in our conversation and told me he was embarrassed. Carefully, I tried to make him look through the eyes of a teacher. What choices presented themselves? Situations happen; what do you need to consider and how do you handle them? We gave him space.

Michael had told his family immediately about the obstacles he had encountered and they were a great support for him. In the third week he shared his story in a peer group meeting with other students. He showed his embarrassment alongside his courage to continue.

Michael undertook little or no initiative in his school-based learning, but he kept coming to school. It seemed as if he wanted to prove something to others and himself. On the other hand, his proactivity was gone; he wasn't coping. The SBTE and I discussed how Michael was dealing with what had happened to him. We prepared ourselves for the impending conversation with him. The question was how we could get him to move on. We decided to start from his experience. He has to be able to deal with dilemmas that arise for teachers today. The school has more pupils than those involved in the upheaval that overwhelmed Michael. A teacher also provides a contribution to social values in addition to taking care of classes. The reality demands immediate action, the responsibility to honour existing commitments and to take up tasks again. We agreed to give him the space he needed but to continue to expect him to make progress in his learning. As a stepping-stone, we came up with a question about his proactivity in workplace learning: what are you going to do and how are you going to finish this placement?

Michael was on time and was looking for us in the SBTE's room. Something had changed; with some amazement he shared the conversation that he'd had with the pupil involved, her parents and the year leader, as part of the investigation. He expressed his admiration for the approach of the year leader. In this conversation Michael had developed, he'd experienced a sort of understanding for the pupil involved. 'I don't know why, but by seeing how the parents dealt with their child in this conversation, I saw that there was much more to it with this pupil', he told us. Suddenly he became aware of a different perspective than his own. This, in turn, brought positive energy with it. We all looked at each other, happy and full of expectation. I responded to Michael's experience: 'That's good; what are you going to do now?' He answered confidently: 'Finish my placement!'

Michael completed his placement. The about-turn that he'd experienced demonstrated that he'd taken ownership of his learning.

CRITICAL QUESTIONS

Identifying strategies and learning from challenges

» Read the story and consider together how this student was able to develop personally and professionally through this experience.

» Where did the challenge arise for the IBTE?

» How did the teacher educator approach the challenge?

» What strategies did he/she use? How did these strategies work?

» What was the significant learning for the IBTE and for the student?

» Reflect on your learning from this story and on the activity.

TEACHER EDUCATOR STORY 4.3

Read through this story and see what teacher educator dilemma(s) you can spot.

When I was giving some induction for the next year's cohort, and the students were discussing a learning point in groups, a panic-stricken colleague called me over and asked if I had a minute to help.

In the office, one of our current students – Kate – was sitting slumped at a computer in tears, having walked out of a nearby lecture about preparing for the next year as a newly qualified teacher. Colleagues were uneasy about how to help.

PROFESSIONALISM AND WELL-BEING

> *We went outside the building and sat on the grass in the sunshine. She proceeded to talk about the situation which she had been facing recently. This situation had brought about uncontrollably strong emotions for Kate and she felt overwhelmed with emotion and unable to stay for the rest of the lecture.*
>
> *She apologised for taking up my time. I reassured her that this is what I was here for. She spent a long while talking about the highs and lows of the training year, now almost at an end, about the holiday to come and about wishes for next year. We spoke about the passing nature of highs and lows and how even the very lowest lows can pass.*
>
> *Having approached her and **a**ssessed the situation; **l**istened to her outpouring of strong emotion; **g**iven information about sources of support; **e**ncouraged her to continue to seek professional sources of support; and **e**ncouraged her to continue to see the benefit of seeking other sources of support from social circles and from her dog, I realised that what had happened was the running-through of the process of mental health first aid and was time worth spending.*
>
> *As usual, we arranged a follow-up time to meet and see how things were going and she left in a considerably calmer state than when she had needed to leave the lecture.*
>
> *She is still teaching high-quality lessons in her employing school, looking forward to Master's research and developing her teaching over the next few years with the support of her colleagues in school. She is lucky to be working in a school where the headteacher, induction colleagues and teaching team recognise the importance of emotional well-being. And they know they are lucky to have her.*
>
> *As for Kate, life is not always easy. She has ongoing access to support from us and from local support services. She speaks confidently and with overwhelmingly positive feedback to large audiences involved in education regarding the importance of increased mental health awareness. This is what keeps her going.*

CRITICAL QUESTIONS

Issues and outcomes

» When you read through the story, identify the main issue that strikes you and the outcome that is associated with that issue.

» What do you think about the outcome? Could it have been improved in any way for the participants in the story?

» Consider situations that you are aware of in which student mental health has been an issue, and how it has been dealt with. Are there lessons to learn?

The Mental Health First Aid Action Plan in England (MHFA, 2020) uses the acronym ALGEE, which stands for:

Assess for risk of suicide or harm

Listen non-judgmentally

Give reassurance and information

Encourage appropriate professional help

Encourage self-help and other support strategies

This is indicated in Story 4.3 through the use of bold letters.

» Could you use this first aid action plan with teacher educators in your partnership?

» What other resources and professional help are available through your schools and university for students and for teacher educators?

» Is any further training needed?

COACHING QUESTIONS

How can you prepare students for the challenges they may experience regarding safeguarding themselves, as well as pupils? (Story 4.2)

When an issue arises with student professionalism, what strategies do you have that could help? Are there ways that you can explicitly model professional attitudes and behaviour? (Story 4.1)

What impact are well-being issues having on your practice? How is well-being embedded into your weekly mentoring conversations? How can you enrich your own practice, and help to develop the practice of others with respect to looking after the well-being of students and colleagues? (Story 4.3)

REFLECTIONS

Sometimes challenges arise internally due to conflicts between the professional, personal and situational dimensions of our identity and sometimes externally due to the behaviour of others. When we experience a challenge that has arisen externally, with students or colleagues, it is helpful to identify where the issue lies, in order to formulate possible solution(s). Maybe the problem lies with their professional attitude; public conduct; another aspect of the professional standards; safeguarding; or well-being. Likewise, when we experience a challenge that causes internal conflict, it is important to take time to examine where the issue lies and what would help us to deal with the issue effectively, realising that internal conflicts can be cognitive or emotional. Recognising and learning how to handle challenges that do not have resolutions is all part of our professional growth and development.

As our professional knowledge and understanding increases, we will need to develop our practice individually and collectively with respect to supporting our health, safety and well-being. In times of change, collaborative professional learning and development become even more important both within partnerships and between partnerships, nationally and internationally, in order to contribute to improving the teacher education profession, and to be informed, constructive advocates for high-quality education for all learners.

Policymakers value competency-based models for teacher education, trying to capture the essence of a good teacher in a list of skills and focusing on outcomes. Some of the problems of a competency-based approach are fragmentation of the teacher's role; separation from the specific context in which the teacher is working; and limitation to measurable qualities rather than personal attributes such as enthusiasm, adaptability, or love of young people. To broaden our discussion to a more integrated model that embraces competencies, personal growth and the context in which we work, the 'onion model' may be helpful (Korthagen, 2004). Imagine an onion cut in half, so that you can see the layers, travelling into the core. This represents the various levels at which students (also teachers and teacher educators) can be influenced. These levels are interacting. The outer levels (environment and behaviour) are observable, and therefore attract the most attention from students who tend to focus on challenges in their classes and question how to deal with these challenges. The third level (travelling towards the centre of the onion) is that of competencies, the statutory knowledge and skills required for professional qualification. It will depend on the circumstances as to whether the competencies are enacted in behaviour. The opportunity to practise behaviour in school helps students to develop the competency to apply this behaviour in other educational contexts.

Beliefs are the fourth level. It is important to examine our beliefs about teaching and learning because they influence our behaviour and our competency. We come into the profession after many years as pupils in school developing our own beliefs about teaching, which may conflict with the principles behind the initial teacher education curriculum adopted by the partnership, for example, a transmission model of teaching compared to a constructivist model. How we see our professional identity is the fifth level within the onion: changes here do not take place easily. The sixth level, at the centre of the onion, is our mission, motivation, ideals or purpose.

The implication of this for teacher education is that there are interventions that are appropriate for change at each of these levels that might provide personalised support for students. At the first level, consideration needs to be given to creating a suitable learning environment for the student and whether the school and/or department/age phase has capacity for nurturing the development of a student. Behaviour, the second level, can be explicitly modelled and unhelpful actions can be identified, and alternatives learnt. Helpful actions are also recognised and positively rewarded. Competencies can be taught through theory and practice with coaching. In order to progress, we need to address the deeper levels of our beliefs about learning and teaching, our developing professional identity, and our core mission. These levels might be more helpfully addressed by using stories of challenges in practice alongside other colleagues. Reflection on these stories can help to surface our beliefs, so they can be challenged and different concepts considered, and can help us to acquire a greater awareness of the levels of our professional identity and mission. This may, in turn, support the development of our individual and collective resilience (Gu and Day, 2013). Some of the stories may be helpful to use with students, for this deeper level of reflection around their professional development. Additionally, you might decide that it is helpful to collect stories of students' challenges in practice to use for this purpose. Chapter 7 will provide more guidance on developing your own stories.

Further resources

Greer, J and Daly, C (2019) *Professionally Acceptable Workload: A Second UCET Companion*. [online] Available at: www.ucet.ac.uk/11213/professionally-acceptable-workload-a-second-ucet-companion-october-2019 (accessed 6 February 2021).

The culture of extreme workload in pursuit of perpetual improvement is embedded in a whole generation of teachers. The Department for Education (DfE, 2018) has taken steps to emphasise the importance of addressing excessive teacher workload, in order to reduce the number of teachers leaving the profession and to encourage more entrants to teaching. This paper is in response to the guidance, to encourage teacher education partnerships to talk frankly about their beliefs about working long hours, so that more teachers, including new entrants, come to believe that a teaching career is sustainable.

Mental Health First Aid International. [online] Available at: www.mhfainternational.org/why-mhfa.html (accessed 6 February 2021).

Mental Health First Aid (MHFA) was first developed in Australia, with the aim of increasing the mental health literacy of the Australian community. But today, MHFA is an international public health programme that has been adapted by several countries. The standard MHFA course teaches techniques to assist someone who is developing a mental health problem or experiencing a mental health crisis before seeking professional help.

References

Beijaard, D, Meijer, P C and Verloop, N (2004) Reconsidering Research on Teachers' Professional Identity. *Teaching and Teacher Education*, 20(2): 107–28.

Day, C and Kington, A (2008) Identity, Well-being and Effectiveness: The Emotional Contexts of Teaching. *Pedagogy, Culture and Society*, 16(1): 7–23.

Day, C, Kington, A, Stobart, G and Sammons, P (2006) The Personal and Professional Selves of Teachers: Stable and Unstable Identities. *British Educational Research Journal*, 32(4): 601–16.

Department for Education (DfE) (2018) *Addressing Teacher Workload in Initial Teacher Education (ITE)*. [online] Available at: www.gov.uk/government/publications/addressing-workload-in-initial-teacher-education-ite (accessed 6 February 2021).

Greer, J and Daly, C (2019) *Professionally Acceptable Workload: A Second UCET Companion*. [online] Available at: www.ucet.ac.uk/11213/professionally-acceptable-workload-a-second-ucet-companion-october-2019 (accessed 6 February 2021).

Gu, Q and Day, C (2013) Challenges to Teacher Resilience: Conditions Count. *British Educational Research Journal*, 39(1): 22–44. https://doi.org/10.1080/01411926.2011.623152

Korthagen, F A J (2004) In Search of the Essence of a Good Teacher: Towards a More Holistic Approach in Teacher Education. *Teaching and Teacher Education*, 20: 77–97.

Lave, J and Wenger, E (1991) *Situated Learning: Legitimate Peripheral Participation*. Cambridge: Cambridge University Press.

Mental Health First Aid England (MHFA) (2020) Online Mental Health Training. [online] Available at: https://mhfaengland.org/ (accessed 6 February 2021).

CHAPTER 5 | QUALITY OF PROVISION

KEY **THEMES**

This chapter is about:
- *the quality assurance of initial teacher education;*
- *mentor learning and development;*
- *the development of school-based teacher educators who are supervising teacher education in their school or a cluster of schools.*

TEACHER EDUCATOR **STORIES**

Teacher educator story 5.1 is written by a lead school-based teacher educator for a group of schools about training mentors.

Teacher educator story 5.2 is written by a school-based teacher educator about monitoring quality of mentoring.

Teacher educator story 5.3 is written by a school-based teacher educator about quality assuring the mentoring relationship.

Teacher educator and mentoring development

Teacher educators are instrumental to the development of early career teachers; therefore, it is vital to support their professional learning and development. One of the challenges around teacher education is the variability in quality of support provided by school-based mentoring (DfE, 2015), leading to the introduction of the *National Standards for School-Based Initial Teacher Training (ITT) Mentors* (DfE, 2016). They provide a framework for the professional development of mentors with the aspiration to raise the profile of mentoring and support the development of a sense of identity for mentors; and to build a coaching and mentoring culture in schools. Mentors are expected to take responsibility for developing their personal qualities; mentoring skills to guide students in their teaching and professionalism; and building a good relationship with colleagues working in the partnership (see Chapter 6). With the introduction of the *ITT Core Content Framework* (DfE, 2019), there is a minimum requirement that students receive clear, consistent and effective mentoring with structured feedback, using the best available evidence. This expectation highlights the need to address issues of teacher educators' knowledge, skills, attributes and identities, and particularly their professional development.

Planning for relevant and appropriate professional development with a diverse group of teacher educators is a challenge, and much of the professional learning will come from the interplay between their practical wisdom from prior experience; feedback from students and other evaluations of the programme; the public knowledge obtained from research and reviews; and the opportunity to reflect together on how this comes together around the issues that teacher educators are facing in their own context (Boyd et al, 2015). Story 5.1 provides insight into leading mentor development within your school, alliance or partnership.

Quality assurance

The fifth principle for initial teacher education partnerships that Mutton et al (2018) propose is to have high levels of quality assurance to ensure consistency, equity and compliance. In initial teacher education, quality assurance takes place on many levels, from recruitment and selection to school-based practice; from that which is happening on the ground to that which happens in programme development. Programme development relies on regular evaluation which takes account of the views of all stakeholders, including the students; aims and outcomes; admissions and performance data. Throughout there are national regulatory requirements that must be met, which rely on good programme management and administration. The aspect of quality assurance that lends itself to examination using stories of challenges in practice is the oversight of the programme on the ground – ensuring that quality is maintained at all levels, so that students have an equitable experience that meets their professional learning needs and provides access to the full range of learning opportunities. This requires individual plans with careful consideration of the affordance that is given in the different contexts for the school-based experience. In many cases, mentors are the gatekeepers to these opportunities, making it important that mentor development includes an understanding of the specific learning opportunities that the workplace can afford (see Chapter 2). Monitoring and 'mentoring the mentors' are usually carried out by an SBTE who supervises the school-based training of students within a school or across an alliance of schools. This role can be daunting for newcomers, and specific professional development for this role is an important consideration in partnerships. An experienced buddy can be a useful mentor for someone new to this role. It can be helpful to bring together these SBTEs to form a professional learning community where research can be shared, good practice disseminated and challenges in practice explored. This also helps the professional identity of SBTEs to develop and the ethos of the partnership to be shared and owned. This has a critical impact on quality assurance. Teacher educator stories 5.2 and 5.3 could be helpfully used together with a group of SBTEs to discuss how to monitor, quality assure and improve the quality of mentoring. These stories illustrate two different approaches, and there may be other ways to resolve these situations too. Sharing together can help you to consider your approach, and even to develop guidance to use within your partnership for deciding when to use which course of action.

TEACHER EDUCATOR **STORY 5.1**

Read through this story and see what teacher educator dilemma(s) you can spot.

When I became a school-based teacher educator (SBTE), supervising the training of teachers in my school alliance, it soon became clear to me that the mentor has a great impact in school-based training. When that mentor has an open mind, has space, gives to the student, and wants to learn together with the student, then it's a rich learning environment for the student. The university set up training for mentors, where all mentors involved in school-based teacher education were obliged to attend. The content was diverse: information about the curriculum and about coaching, and from practising coaching skills with a training actor to coaching the student. In my eyes it was what was needed; the mentors themselves, however, thought differently. Even though the training was judged good enough on the evaluation forms, we heard rumours that the training was insufficiently in line with the mentors' wishes. What to do? We really wanted to involve the mentors actively in school-based teacher education. It was a challenge for us as a project team. How could we provide training in which mentors really got motivated and came to learn?

We had to make some changes. We organised it differently; from four whole days we went back to two afternoons and we picked out those elements that really seemed to matter and where the highest rating came. It felt good to make an adjustment that would benefit the mentors in our eyes. We missed the mark again. The discontent was repeated; mentors didn't feel intrinsically involved in the training and only came to it because they had to.

Then I got the opportunity to take it over, and I grabbed it with both hands. It was a challenge for me and I knew I could learn a lot from it. It was also a task in which my voice would have a greater reach.

The first thing I did was to talk about it with the co-ordinator of the university and he came up with a valuable tip: talk with the mentors! Ask them why they don't feel involved in this training. And that is what I did! I talked with the mentors themselves, but also with their school leaders, with the SBTEs overseeing the training in their schools and other key people involved. This clarified a lot. The mentors didn't need another training session with a lot of things they'd learnt in other professional development courses, at a time of heavy workload in just doing their jobs and having to travel to the university for it! The training felt more like a burden than an interesting learning encounter. They told me they needed exchange with other mentors; they wanted to learn more about the curriculum and solution-oriented coaching was high on the wish list.

I went back to the university and they listened to my findings. How nice it felt to be taken so seriously. They gave me the space for an experiment in collaboration with the university. What if we start a pilot with a 'mentoring workshop' with a group of schools? No training, but a time of being together in which we work together and learn together. Not at the university but simply at one of the schools; that saves travel time. A workshop like this gives space to respond to what's happening within their own schools. What are the challenges; what do these mentors want to learn? We also organised the workshop to include the institute-based teacher educators (IBTEs) who were working with these schools. Together, we came up with practical workshops with meaningful content, for example, about the assessment form: how do you assess? When I fill in a four-point scale on an assessment form, what does that 4 mean for me? And what does 4 mean for you? Is that the same for every mentor? Just talking about this together proved to be very useful.

I found this pilot that we started exciting! How would the mentors receive this new way of working? Would they open up? I decided to put my own uncertainties aside and just do it. Experimentation is part of daring. And it worked! The mentors felt heard and enjoyed meeting each other. They felt appreciated by the university because now the IBTE joined the sessions in the schools, instead of the other way around.

This success means that next year we are going to scale up. No more training at the university; workshops in the schools now. No more standard training but responding to the questions of those mentors within those schools. Fully customised. That models what we want when we educate students together: a student who can work from his/her own learning questions and not from a curriculum imposed from above.

And what have I learnt? That experimenting is an exciting, but especially useful, step in finding out what works and what doesn't work. It creates an open attitude in which we dare to look more broadly and therefore can connect much more to the needs that existed, but which we didn't anticipate. But, above all, that we shouldn't talk about students or mentors, but we should talk with them! When they feel taken seriously and we really listen to them, they get much more out of their comfort zone and they dare to show where they want to grow. We are not just teaching, but we are learning together!

CRITICAL **QUESTIONS**

Key words

» Use different colours and highlight the significant words in the story for you.

» Discuss the story in pairs or triplets. What's it all about?

» What is the significance of your key words? Are they different from those chosen by others?

» Reflect on your learning from this story and the activity.

TEACHER EDUCATOR **STORY 5.2**

Read through this story and see what teacher educator dilemma(s) you can spot.

I am writing as a school-based teacher educator (SBTE) who supervises the students within my school. In the fifth year of being an SBTE, Debbie, a young student, started with us. Debbie seemed to be eager and interested but lacked confidence and was quite defensive when receiving feedback. Her mentor, an experienced teacher and brilliant mentor, had very specific expectations. These included things such as: going through lesson plans; discussing all taught lessons in mentor meetings; giving written feedback on all lessons; and the student using their own strategies to improve their practice rather than relying on being given 'the answers'. These are all strategies and ways to help students progress and be reflective practitioners. This proved very difficult for Debbie. She would often get upset and feel under enormous pressure to complete all the things being asked of her.

Considering these anxieties, the mentor found it difficult to tackle targets and ways to progress for Debbie and they seemed to hit a stalemate. When the mentor gave Debbie more than one target, she would complain that she was given too much to do and no advice on how to achieve the targets being set. She also objected to the written feedback as she saw it as being formally assessed after each lesson rather than seeing that the notes were intended to be supportive.

From the mentor's point of view, Debbie was moving too slowly and she was frustrated that the same targets seemed to be being set week upon week.

I then stepped in. It was true: Debbie was moving particularly slowly and was deflecting any comments or advice that the mentor was giving because she felt as though the mentor was being unreasonable. Each thing that was offered was declined or an excuse was given as to why she could not take the advice. From the mentor's perspective, Debbie was being stubborn and unco-operative. We agreed between us that a decision had to be made. Debbie was told to take some time to really consider her options and think about how she could approach the rest of her training and be more proactive (if she wanted to continue).

I suggested a change of mentor.

This really worked. We saw an instant change in Debbie's attitude and approach to her training. She was less obstructive and more proactive in her practice and seemed to respond to (the same) targets with a different and more positive energy. There are still issues such as behaviour and pace of lesson but Debbie has just been graded a 2 where, two months ago, I had doubts that she would finish the course.

CRITICAL **QUESTIONS**

Critical incidents

A *'critical incident is one that challenges your own assumptions or makes you think differently'* (McAteer et al, 2010, p 107).

» Read through the story. This stalemate was a critical incident identified by the SBTE that was significant to their professional learning. Identify the triggers that caused the stalemate.

» What options could have been available to overcome the stalemate?

» What other consequences could have arisen from the course of action taken?

» Reflect on your learning from this story and the activity.

McAteer et al (2010, p 107) provide the following helpful prompts to guide reflection on critical incidents:

» 'What happened and where and when?' Give a brief history of the incident.

» What is it that has made the incident 'critical'?

» What were your immediate thoughts and responses?

» What are your thoughts now? What has changed/developed your thinking?

» What have you learnt about (your) practice from this?

» How might your practice change and develop as a result of this analysis and learning?

Using these prompts, do you think that this story is about a critical incident? Why/Why not?

Consider your own practice; does a critical incident come to mind? Try using these prompts to help you to reflect on the critical incident. An example of how these prompts can be used is included in the further resources section at the end of the chapter.

TEACHER EDUCATOR **STORY 5.3**

Read through this story and see what teacher educator dilemma(s) you can spot.

This academic year, as the school-based teacher educator (SBTE), I had three school-led students in my school to supervise their training. Two of them made excellent and rapid progress and one, while making progress, was slower in his grasp and competency of the Teachers' Standards.

The teacher mentor was becoming frustrated that while Simon was receptive to feedback, the impact was marginal and similar targets were ongoing.

The first term we kept the timetable to eight hours with the first four weeks of term being dominated by observation and team teaching before moving into collaborative planning and finally the student taking the lead for all eight hours by the Christmas break. As SBTE I needed to remind the teacher mentor that this was normal… a guy off the street with no experience of teaching being able to plan and deliver eight hours a week and generally achieve the learning outcomes for most students was progress. No, he wasn't differentiating effectively or embedding formative assessment but these were much more advanced training priorities to be addressed in the second term. I jointly observed one of Simon's lessons and as a non-specialist put a focus on pedagogy and planning. In our debrief, the teacher mentor highlighted where stretch could have been added or tasks done differently and while I acknowledged this was important I kept drawing the conversation back to 'Did the students make progress as a result of Simon's planning, teaching, resourcing and questioning?' She answered 'Yes' and so at the end of the first assessment point we agreed the student was making steady progress with clear areas for development. A grade 3 was awarded but with measurable targets of what to do to achieve a 2 by the next assessment.

Simon went to the second school and again I suggested that we both visit him to see how he was progressing in a new context. The teacher mentor really enjoyed this experience and found it interesting to see how another school was delivering Spanish to 11 to 14 year-olds. There was a distinct contrast in the pedagogical style and so with this direct comparison the teacher mentor stated that Simon had clearly moved forward in his practice. There was no longer the 'I would have done' aspect to feedback. A grade 2 was given at the end of the second assessment point.

> *On return to the home school, Simon was still encountering issues with differentiation and assessment of learning, which had been targets for over a term. The teacher mentor approached me, saying they didn't know what else to say so together we created a list of three strategies that we wanted to see embedded in Simon's lessons, every week, across classes. By scaling back and focusing explicitly on these standards, we hoped Simon would feel he could address these concerns. All observations leading up to the final visit by the university tutor saw these targets being met. In preparation for the final assessment, the teacher mentor and I met to moderate the final grade. The teacher mentor was still unsure if Simon had completely secured a grade 2 and so we sat with a highlighter and a profile provided by the university of what an outstanding student looks like. We discussed each statement in relation to Simon and highlighted where he was consistently meeting this statement. At the end of our discussion, about 70 per cent of the profile was highlighted. I asked the teacher mentor what this meant, to which she replied: 'Well, he's definitely good'. The areas that remained un-highlighted naturally formed targets for the NQT year and we could confidently grade the student a 2 overall with aspects of outstanding. These targets were focused on curriculum knowledge, use of data and the wider professional role.*

CRITICAL QUESTIONS

Positive feedback

» Read the story and discuss how you think the SBTE feels and what concerns you think he/she has, at each stage of the story.

» What positive feedback would you give him/her?

» How do you think the mentor feels and what concerns do you think she has at each stage? What positive feedback can you give her?

» How do you think the student might complete the sentence beginning 'It was helpful when you…'?

» Reflect on your learning from this story and on participating in the activity. Share with the group.

COACHING QUESTIONS

How can you foster opportunities to talk with students and mentors to understand their needs? (Story 5.1)

How can you use programme documentation to support the individual professional learning of mentors and students? Are there changes in your approach or in the documentation that would help? (Story 5.3)

How can you approach the issue of changing a mentor so that each person involved can feel valued and use it as an opportunity for professional learning? (Story 5.2)

REFLECTIONS

One of the ways that mentors are encouraged to develop their practice is by engaging with the best available evidence (DfE, 2016). The professional learning of teacher educators lies in the interplay between practical wisdom, which may be informal and situated within the partnership, and formal public knowledge, which includes theory, research and policy (Boyd et al, 2015). Teacher educators need to move beyond the pragmatic evaluation of everyday quality assurance procedures to being actively engaged in professional inquiry or practitioner research (Boyd and White, 2017). At the level of pragmatic evaluation there will be some engagement with public knowledge, in the form of professional guidance and policy documents. When engaged in professional inquiry, teacher educators critically analyse professional guidance and research evidence and consider the interplay of this knowledge with practice. Practitioner research takes this further; being informed by critical review of the literature, teacher educators may develop their own theoretical framework with which to analyse practice (Boyd and White, 2017).

In the published literature on teacher education, the emerging themes over the last decade include research about and by teacher educators, schools–university teacher education partnerships, knowledge of teacher educators' work and professional development. Research is becoming an increasingly important part of the work of being a teacher educator, with teacher educators engaged in researching to improve their understanding and practice and sharing their research and having a growing voice.

Teacher educators have increased in both number and diversity but also in recognition of the value of their work, and in a qualitative sense individually and as a professional community (White and Swennen, 2020).

Further resources

Birmingham City University (nd) Example Critical Incident Reflections. [online] Available at: www.crec.co.uk/_literature_138397/BCU_-_Example_Critical_Incident_Reflection (accessed 6 February 2021).

This is an example of reflecting on a critical incident.

InFo-TED (2019) *The Importance of Teacher Educators: Professional Development Imperatives*. White paper. [online] Available at: https://info-ted.eu/wp-content/uploads/2019/10/InFo-TED-White-Paper.pdf (accessed 6 February 2021).

This paper highlights the need for governmental support for teacher educator induction and further professional development in EU countries because educational improvement through reforms and structural changes requires equal attention to be given to the professional development of the teacher educators who lead in mediating these reforms.

Jones, K and White, E (2014) Developing Outstanding Practice in School-based Teacher Education. In Menter, I (ed) *Critical Guides for Teacher Educators*. Northwich: Critical Publishing.

The first part of this book challenges teacher educators to ask critical questions about their personal and professional development. The second part provides critical questions to develop the quality of provision with examples of evaluating impact drawn from a variety of settings.

Lorist, P and Swennen, A (2016) *Life and Work of Teacher Educators* (P Lorist and A Swennen, eds, Vol 2). HU University of Applied Sciences. [online] Available at: https://issuu.com/hogeschoolutrecht/docs/itt_life_and_work_of_teacher_educators (accessed on 6 February 2021).

This booklet contains the stories of nine teacher educators from around the world, discussing how they became teacher educators and their work and professional development.

NASBTT (nd) Teacher Educator and Mentoring Zone (TEMZ). [online] Available at: www.nasbtt.org.uk/temz/ (accessed 6 February 2021).

The National Association of School-Based Teacher Trainers (NASBTT) supports, develops and empowers mentors by providing accessible guidance in key areas of mentoring summarised in the *Professional Framework for Teacher Educators*. The content is built on existing theory and research around practice. The zone is evolving as relevant resources, links to articles, further reading and videos are being added. Membership is required for access.

Swennen, A and White, E (2020) *Being a Teacher Educator: Research-Informed Methods for Improving Practice*. Abingdon: Taylor & Francis.

The chapters in this book support the research-informed improvement of different aspects of teacher educators' work, such as pedagogy, curriculum development, mentoring, research supervision and their own professional development. The aim of the book is to foster the voice of teacher educators and support teacher educators to strive towards a greater visibility of their contributions to national and international initiatives for high-quality teacher education.

References

Boyd, P, Hymer B and Lockney, K (2015) *Learning Teaching: Becoming an Inspirational Teacher*. Northwich: Critical Publishing.

Boyd, P and White, E (2017) Teacher Educator Professional Inquiry in an Age of Accountability. In Boyd, P and Szplit, A (eds) *Teachers and Teacher Educators Learning Through Inquiry: International Perspectives*. Kraków: Attyka. [online] Available at: http://researchprofiles.herts.ac.uk/portal/files/12126690/Teacher_Educator_Professional_Inquiry_in_an_Age_of_Accountability._Boyd_White_2017.pdf (accessed 6 February 2021).

Department for Education (DfE) (2015) *Carter Review of Initial Teacher Training*. [online] Available at: www.gov.uk/government/publications/carter-review-of-initial-teacher-training (accessed 6 February 2021).

Department for Education (DfE) (2016) *National Standards for School-Based Initial Teacher Training (ITT) Mentors*. [online] Available at: https://assets.publishing.service.gov.uk/government/uploads/system/uploads/attachment_data/file/536891/Mentor_standards_report_Final.pdf (accessed 6 February 2021).

Department for Education (DfE) (2019) *ITT Core Content Framework*. [online] Available at: www.gov.uk/government/publications/initial-teacher-training-itt-core-content-framework (accessed 6 February 2021).

McAteer, M, Hallett, F, Murtagh, L and Turnbull, G (2010) *Achieving your Master's in Teaching and Learning*. Exeter: Learning Matters.

Mutton, T, Burn, K, Hagger, H and Thirlwell, K (2018) *Teacher Education Partnerships: Policy and Practice*. St Albans: Critical Publishing.

White, E and Swennen A (2020) Introduction to Being a Teacher Educator: Research-Informed Methods for Improving Practice. In Swennen, A and White, E (eds) *Being a Teacher Educator: Research-Informed Methods for Improving Practice*. London: Routledge.

CHAPTER 6 | USING THE STORIES COLLABORATIVELY

> **KEY THEMES**
>
> This chapter is about:
> - *using the stories as part of collaborative professional development;*
> - *using the stories to develop curriculum design;*
> - *using the stories to develop leadership;*
> - *using the stories in relation to the Mentor Standards and other professional frameworks for teacher educators.*

Collaborative professional development

These autobiographical stories express the perspectives of individual teacher educators on challenges they have experienced in their practice and enable us to participate vicariously in other realities than our own. Reading stories can change our perceptions, leading to changes in our actions in the real world. Jarvis and Graham (2015) use a metaphor of putting on shoes to illustrate how stories can be used to help us to examine different perspectives, to stand in the shoes of others, and to examine our own shoes more carefully. By constructing the world that other stakeholders in our partnerships experience – students, mentors and others – within our own imaginations, we can start to understand how we can make that world better (Jarvis and Trodd, 2008). By using stories for collaborative professional development, we can have the informative insights of others from their perspectives, rather than relying on our own imaginations, to aid us in interpreting the stories.

When stories are used in professional development workshops, participants in the workshops can learn about the social world with a high degree of attention while feeling relaxed about the experience. Information may be absorbed more easily than factual information relayed in a lecture (Jarvis and Graham, 2015). The interpretive approach of exploring stories together can help us to realise why some stakeholders in partnerships behave in particular ways. Having mixed groups of teacher educators from schools and universities together within a partnership can be very helpful for exploring challenging issues that are difficult to surface. By stepping outside of the experience and looking at it together, questions can be asked genuinely from an inquiry stance rather than in a threatening and judgemental way. This can enhance practice and relationships within the partnership.

In one example of using the stories in a professional development workshop with groups of teacher educators from schools and universities across different partnerships, some groups were mixed, while some groups were all teacher educators based in schools or all teacher educators based in one university. The experience of those in mixed groups was very positive, as genuine professional learning took place as they were able to explore issues in practice outside of the processes of their own partnership, yet from the perspectives of each of the different actors in the story. Learning also took place where the teacher educators were all school based yet came from different schools and partnerships which were working in different ways. The group which had participants who were all based in the same university found the workshop disappointing. They were aware that they did not gain as much professional learning because they had to imagine themselves in the shoes of the different actors in the story without the insights of others in the group who could more easily relate to the other perspectives.

It is important to realise that sometimes we mean different things when we use the same words, especially when we are working across institutional or international boundaries. You may need to change some of the terminology within the stories before you use them, so that the teacher educators that you are working with recognise the different actors and feel comfortable with the stories. Alternatively, you may want to consider the terminology within the story you are using and translate it together into the terminology you use within your settings (see the Glossary).

If you are leading professional development using the stories, you will find it useful to draw on research- and practice-informed guidance on how to lead professional development sessions with teachers and teacher educators in order to maximise the professional learning. Mynott (2017) writes helpfully in his thesis about the need for cognitive dissonance to change attitudes and to enable professional learning, and for those leading professional development to be able to enable the participants to stay within that zone of professional conflict for long enough for their currently held theories to be challenged and for their thinking to be transformed. He found that the presence of dissonance itself was not sufficient to progress professional conflict to a learning opportunity. There was a need for sustained dissonance leading into discontinuity and then potentially into a learning opportunity. These stories, together with the critical questions, may be a helpful tool to generate and sustain cognitive dissonance by providing a group of teacher educators a focus on practice, away from the awkwardness of focusing on the practice of any one individual within the group. By sharing an understanding of the need for sustained dissonance for professional learning, the group may be able to embrace the discomfort for the sake of learning professionally and improving practice.

The dominant culture of the partnership will also impact on the extent to which new ideas can be explored, with possible transformation of practice. The prevailing culture may embrace conflict and difference, and thereby support professional learning, or it may actively seek to expel difference for the sake of group consensus, taking an avoidant stance (Achinstein, 2002). You may find it helpful to consider together with others in your partnership where your partnership lies on a trajectory from avoidance of conflict to embracing conflict. In some areas of your practice you may find you have developed a more open and explorative culture than in other areas.

A teacher education partnership can be described as a community of practice, where a group of individuals are working together towards a shared purpose and learning together how to do it better (Wenger, 1998). Within these communities of practice, we develop shared language, procedures and our identities as teacher educators. There is a deep link between identity and practice, and we negotiate our identities as teacher educators within the community of practice. If we move into a new partnership, we may move into a new community of practice. Having developed our identity within our original professional context, we will need to develop new identities, including different ways of working, yet retain the specialist knowledge and skills that we bring to the team. Developing a new identity within a new team is professionally challenging, involving the retention of expertise while embracing different ways of working and developing shared practice. When we recognise the significance of our community of practice to our development, whether we are new to the partnership or an established member, we realise the importance of prioritising quality time for collaborative professional development, where we can work alongside each other and learn together.

CRITICAL **QUESTIONS**

After you have used a story as part of a collaborative professional development opportunity, you will find it helpful to extend your learning individually or together using these prompts:

» Reflect on your learning from the story – what have you learnt?

» Reflect on participating in the activity – what have you learnt?

» Share your learning with the group.

» How will you use this learning to develop your practice?

Using the stories to develop curriculum design

In Chapter 1 we thought about how the initial teacher education curriculum can be developed so that the learning opportunities provided to students during their school experience support their development appropriately. We used Story 2.2 to consider who should be involved in planning these learning opportunities and how they can dovetail with the professional learning that the student is engaging with on their course. The *ITT Core Content Framework* (DfE, 2019) provides a minimum entitlement for students that must be embraced within the curriculum that the partnership designs. Story 3.2 also challenges us regarding the clarity that teacher educators and mentors on the ground have about where the responsibility for different aspects of the curriculum lie. Mutton et al (2018) have clearly defined roles and responsibilities within the partnership as their fourth principle for initial teacher education partnerships. These roles and responsibilities will need to be constantly part of your dialogue.

Wherever we find boundaries have become blurred because of changes in personnel, context or policy, there is a need for listening, connecting and clear communication, which can be facilitated by using a narrative approach.

The mix of academic and practical coverage in the curriculum prompts the need for collaborative curriculum development, which may be led by the university or central base of the partnership but needs to be owned at every level of the partnership and in every setting. Building knowledge (learn that…) and experience (learn how to…) involves providing theoretical and practical tools and developing dispositions. This is a huge challenge. The way we work together in our partnership using the strengths of teacher educators in the school and university is key and can be examined using Stories 3.1, 5.1, 5.2 and 5.3.

It is important to provide an opportunity for all stakeholders in your teacher education provision to have a voice in the development of the curriculum in order to ensure that it provides students with the breadth of experience and understanding that they will need to develop as a professional who can work confidently in diverse settings. You can use Story 3.3 as a prompt to consider how to facilitate coverage of the curriculum and the flexibility you need for teaching each group of students. The third principle that Mutton et al (2018) propose is to consider when and how student teachers will develop the adaptability needed for a career in teaching. Realising that we can only work towards goals and celebrate progress in the right direction, and that we are training teachers for the situation now, not the situation as it used to be, really defines the essence of what it is to teach! It is an important message but one that students, teacher educators and other stakeholders have really struggled with during the Covid-19 pandemic.

Using the stories to develop leadership in times of change

Research indicates that having strong beliefs about core purposes and values, and having support from colleagues and leaders, or a combination of these factors, is essential in contributing to the development of individual and collective resilience (Gu and Day, 2013). Developing leadership is important for provision to be sustainable and resilient and is another aspect of our work as professionals that we can explicitly model, as we seek to share our values and vision across the partnership. The first principle for partnerships proposed by Mutton et al (2018) is to have a shared view of what the desired outcomes should be. You may develop your partnership vision in a variety of ways, enabling any and all stakeholders to contribute their ideas, and working together on a final version that everyone can feel genuinely enthusiastic about. After you have launched your partnership vision, you will still need to work constantly to incorporate the vision as part of everything you do, from mentor development and partnership meetings to teaching students and assessment.

In times of change, like the Covid-19 pandemic, to survive we learn to be more agile and resilient. This is done more easily when there is a strong set of core purposes and values embedded within the partnership. This enables us to prepare for new situations. The first questions we ask ourselves are: what are the key messages about our ethos and vision for the students, and how can we get these across effectively with the tools we have available, online or face to face? Letting go of structures that have worked and been refined over many years is challenging, but by repeatedly asking what is the best way to meet the purpose, we can find a way through together.

When we are travelling through unfamiliar territory together, we need to keep reminding our students and colleagues that we are walking alongside them. Students may be training for a new situation that is different from anything previously experienced by their teacher educators, so they need to learn what it means to be a professional in the current situation, not to develop skills that are appropriate for the past. Where things are not possible now, future professional development may be needed as and when new approaches and skills are required.

Using the stories to support mentor development

When using the stories for collaborative professional learning and development for effective mentoring, you may find Table 6.1 useful, where the stories have been cross-referenced with the *National Standards for School-Based Initial Teacher Training (ITT) Mentors* (DfE, 2016) for those working in England.

As a mentor you could work through one of the stories and the related critical questions to stimulate your thinking regarding an aspect of the mentoring standards that you are developing. You may find other mentors in your school or partnership would like to work with you to look at the story and to develop their practice.

As a teacher educator who has responsibility for mentor development in your school or partnership, you may choose a story for a networking session, focusing on a relevant standard where you would like to see practice develop.

Where there is no story that directly links with a mentoring standard, for example, with respect to modelling your practice of planning, teaching and assessing pupils in the class, then Chapter 7 will help you to collect stories of your own that you could use. Likewise, stories of promoting equality and diversity, safeguarding, compliance and time management could be added to your collection.

Table 6.1 The stories cross-referenced to the Mentor Standards

Story	Author	The challenge	Mentor Standards
2.1	Lead SBTE in a school	The tensions of failing a hardworking student who does not meet the standards.	2.1 support the trainee in forming good relationships with pupils, and in developing effective behaviour and classroom management strategies; 2.4 give constructive, clear and timely feedback on lesson observations; 4.1 ensure consistency by working with other mentors and partners to moderate judgements.

Table 6.1 (*Cont.*)

Story	Author	The challenge	Mentor Standards
2.2	IBTE	Providing access to learning opportunities in the workplace.	2.7 resolve in-school issues on the trainee's behalf where they lack the confidence or experience to do so themselves.
2.3	SBTE (mentor)	Being able to support a student to make progress in a new setting.	1.1 be approachable, make time for the trainee, and prioritise meetings and discussions with them; 2.4 give constructive, clear and timely feedback on lesson observations.
3.1	IBTE	Whether the SBTEs would co-operate with the IBTE.	2.5 broker opportunities to observe best practice; 2.9 enable the trainee to access, utilise and interpret robust educational research to inform their teaching.
3.2	SBTE	Having dual roles of coaching and assessing students.	1.3 offer support with integrity, honesty and respect.
3.3	Lead SBTE in a school	Helping students to learn from their workplace experiences.	1.2 use a range of effective interpersonal skills to respond to the needs of the trainee; 1.3 offer support with integrity, honesty and respect; 1.4 use appropriate challenge to encourage the trainee to reflect on their practice.
4.1	IBTE	Leading an assessment conversation professionally, taking account of the student and the colleagues in the school.	1.4 use appropriate challenge to encourage the trainee to reflect on their practice; 2.7 resolve in-school issues on the trainee's behalf where they lack the confidence or experience to do so themselves; 3.1 encourage the trainee to participate in the life of the school and understand its role within the wider community; 3.2 support the trainee in developing the highest standards of professional and personal conduct; 4.1 ensure consistency by working with other mentors and partners to moderate judgements.

Table 6.1 (*Cont.*)

Story	Author	The challenge	Mentor Standards
4.2	IBTE	Helping a student to move on after a difficult issue in school.	1.1 be approachable, make time for the trainee, and prioritise meetings and discussions with them; 3.2 support the trainee in developing the highest standards of professional and personal conduct.
4.3	Lead SBTE in a school	Helping a student who has mental health issues.	1.1 be approachable, make time for the trainee, and prioritise meetings and discussions with them; 1.2 use a range of effective interpersonal skills to respond to the needs of the trainee; 1.3 offer support with integrity, honesty and respect.
5.1	Lead SBTE across group of schools	Providing meaningful mentor training.	4.1 ensure consistency by working with other mentors and partners to moderate judgements; 4.2 continue to develop their own mentoring practice and subject and pedagogical expertise by accessing appropriate professional development and engaging with robust research.
5.2	Lead SBTE in a school	Enabling a student to make progress when they are not taking on board advice from their mentor.	2.7 resolve in-school issues on the trainee's behalf where they lack the confidence or experience to do so themselves.
5.3	Lead SBTE in a school	Helping a mentor to have appropriate expectations of a student.	2.8 enable and encourage the trainee to evaluate and improve their teaching; 4.1 ensure consistency by working with other mentors and partners to moderate judgements.

(DfE, 2016)

COACHING **QUESTIONS**

> When did you last take time to listen to the perspective of others in your partnership – students, colleagues, other SBTEs and IBTEs? How do you respond when they do not share the same perspective on an aspect of practice as you?

> In what ways could you explore concepts such as reflection, partnership and professional development in order to have a deeper shared understanding with others in your professional learning community?

> What has helped you to develop your identity as a teacher educator within your partnership? How can you engage in genuine professional learning within your community of practice?

REFLECTIONS

It is essential to find spaces for learning conversations with colleagues who will support and challenge us in our work. These conversations can transform our thinking and practice and are enriched by drawing on a wide range of literature, even outside our field. It is important to have a collaborative partnership ethos, and this space, sometimes called the third space, in which to work together in democratic and inclusive ways for professional learning (Zeichner, 2010). These hybrid spaces where academic and practitioner knowledge come together allow challenges in practice to be explored safely, without the fear of judgement and relational damage. Sharing together and discussing with other teacher educators can help you to consider how you might approach an issue should it arise, how you would decide which is the best course of action, and whether your partnership has a preferred way of addressing the challenge. It is interesting that, within the stories, many of the teacher educators sought their own solution to the challenges rather than

> discussing them with others in the partnership. This emphasises the need to continually work at developing collaborative opportunities in partnerships, providing space for developing mutual understanding and trusting relationships and for different approaches to be explored together.

Further resources

Jarvis, J and Graham, S (2015) *Innovative Pedagogies Series: 'It's All About the Shoes' Exploring the Perspectives of Others and Ourselves in Teacher Education*. York: Higher Education Academy. [online] Available at: https://uhra.herts.ac.uk/bitstream/handle/2299/17319/joy_jarvis_final_templated_0.pdf?sequence=2 (accessed 6 February 2021).

This is a useful resource which can help teacher educators to develop a curiosity about their own perspectives and the perspectives of others, enabling them to inquire into their assumptions and thinking that underpin their teaching and practice. It is in three parts: 'Exploring shoes', 'Exploring other people's shoes', and 'Looking at our own shoes'. The resource covers exploring ways to identify perspectives; learning how we can try to stand in the shoes of others; and articulating our own ways of looking at the world, developing the courage to challenge and change these.

References

Achinstein, B (2002) *Community, Diversity, and Conflict Among Schoolteachers: The Ties That Blind*. New York: Teachers College Press.

Department for Education (DfE) (2016) *National Standards for School-Based Initial Teacher Training (ITT) Mentors*. [online] Available at: https://assets.publishing.service.gov.uk/government/uploads/system/uploads/attachment_data/file/536891/Mentor_standards_report_Final.pdf (accessed 6 February 2021).

Department for Education (DfE) (2019) *ITT Core Content Framework*. [online] Available at: www.gov.uk/government/publications/initial-teacher-training-itt-core-content-framework (accessed 6 February 2021).

Gu, Q and Day, C (2013) Challenges to Teacher Resilience: Conditions Count. *British Educational Research Journal*, 39(1): 22–44. https://doi.org/10.1080/01411926.2011.623152

Jarvis, J and Graham, S (2015) *Innovative Pedagogies Series: 'It's All About the Shoes' Exploring the Perspectives of Others and Ourselves in Teacher Education*. York: Higher Education Academy. [online] Available at: https://uhra.herts.ac.uk/bitstream/handle/2299/17319/joy_jarvis_final_templated_0.pdf?sequence=2 (accessed 6 February 2021).

Jarvis, J and Trodd, L (2008) Other Ways of Seeing; Other Ways of Being: Imagination as a Tool for Developing Multi-professional Practice for Children with Communication Needs. *Child Language Teaching and Therapy*, 24(2): 211–27. https://doi.org/10.1177/0265659008090295

Mutton, T, Burn, K, Hagger, H and Thirlwell, K (2018) *Teacher Education Partnerships: Policy and Practice*. St Albans: Critical Publishing.

Mynott, J P (2017) *A Primary Head Teacher's Exploration of Lesson Study*. EdD thesis, University of Hertfordshire. [online] Available at: https://uhra.herts.ac.uk/bitstream/handle/2299/18330/14107916%20Mynott%20John%20Final%20Submission.pdf?sequence=1andisAllowed=y (accessed 6 February 2021).

Wenger, E (1998) *Communities of Practice: Learning, Meaning and Identity*. Cambridge: Cambridge University Press.

Zeichner, K (2010) Rethinking the Connections between Campus Courses and Field Experiences in College- and University-based Teacher Education. *Journal of Teacher Education*, 61(1–2): 89–99.

CHAPTER 7 | YOUR OWN STORIES ABOUT PRACTICE

KEY **THEMES**

This chapter is about:
- *how to write stories about practice;*
- *how to support others to write stories about practice;*
- *how to reflect on your own stories about practice, including different tools for reflection.*

Writing stories about practice

Writing stories about practice is a useful activity for teacher educators to carry out for reflection and self-discovery. The 'writing a story about a challenge in your practice' resource will help you write your own story about practice, or you can use it to support others in their writing. You may decide to have a writing retreat for a couple of hours, where you pair up and share some of the things that you are experiencing as challenges and then write your stories together.

Challenges we experience tend to stick in our minds as critical incidents that are worthy of further investigation for the professional learning that we can glean. Sometimes our challenges are also our highlights, as we celebrate the successful solution to a dilemma. However, we may have other highlights that did not present as challenges but are equally worthy of capture and sharing through a narrative approach.

Stories of practice that focus on what has worked well could inform the 'discover' aspect of an 'appreciative inquiry'. Appreciative inquiry is a solution-focused approach to change management, looking at what is working well already and using that as a starting point (Lewis et al, 2011). It begins with stories of success, draws out the good and the positive and ignores stories of failure.

The process follows these steps.

> » Define a clear outcome and ask in what ways can we develop our partnership work to achieve this outcome.
> » Discover the best of what already works.
> » Dream what might be.
> » Design how to achieve the dream.
> » Deliver through an action plan.

Reflecting on stories about practice

'Reflecting on your own story' is about taking our assumptions and critiquing them. Jarvis and Graham (2015, p 13) encourage us to do this because *'our decision-making will be based on what we view as significant and ethical. If we have not explored our own perspectives and tested them within a professional community, then our judgement may be unsound'*. Throughout the day, as professionals, we have to make many quick decisions, drawing on our intuition. We need to understand what underpins our intuition so that our practical wisdom is well grounded (Vokey and Kerr, 2011).

After writing our own stories about practice within our partnership, 'reflecting together on stories of practice' can help us to discover what is happening during critical moments, deepen our understanding and decide what we will do to embed our new ideas. Often, we can champion an idea or theory and believe we are living by that in our practice, but when we examine our practice carefully we might find our theory in action does not match up (Argyris and Schön, 1974). Collaborative opportunities with colleagues who we trust can provide the opportunity to reflect on our own story of practice and surface assumptions and where there are discrepancies between our beliefs and our practice, enabling us to work with more integrity. We each notice different things depending on our prior experience (Mason, 2002).

Writing a story about a challenge in your practice

Writing stories about practice is a useful activity for teacher educators to carry out for reflection and self-discovery. The use of 'storying' of experience is increasing in the field of professional development (Jarvis, 2005). There is no mystery to writing stories as we all tell stories in our daily lives. Unconscious concerns, issues and dilemmas can be revealed through the descriptive process of story writing, raising awareness so they can be examined.

You will probably find that 600 to 700 words are enough to capture the main things that you want to express in your story.

Write a brief story of a specific challenge or dilemma you have faced in your recent practice (using pseudonyms). Include a beginning and a plot and an ending (if you had one!). You could start 'When I was...'.

» What was the real challenge for you? Where did the challenge arise?

» How did you deal with it? How did that work?

This story about a challenge in practice written by a student may be a useful example for you.

TEACHER EDUCATOR STORY 7.1

Dirty Nora

Her brother from Group 6 drops her off, helps her with her coat, gives her the bag and as he walks to his own class he calls out, 'I'll pick you up at 12'. She stands shyly at the door. She is small, she looks around and then walks to the chair with her name: Nora. She is the first one.

'Hello Nora, good morning. Nice to see you.' *She looks at me but says nothing.*

'Don't you want to get a book? Go on then – pick one.'

I get a few books from the pile and hand them to her noticing suddenly how dirty she is. Her clothes are full of stains, and her nose is runny. There is jam on her cheek and what looks like chocolate paste around her mouth. She looks at the books and chooses the top one. It's been ages since she washed her hands and there is snot on her right sleeve.

'Read out loud?' *I hear her ask. I look at her and see two blue eyes with sleep in the corners.* 'Teacher, can you read to me?' *she insists. There is no one in the classroom yet, only the two of us. What should I do? I try and get over my disgust and tell her:* 'Ok, I'll sit with you.'

She beams. I sit next to her and suddenly smell her too. She stinks. You could smell her from a mile off. Suddenly she puts her face on my arm and as I pull it away, I notice her snot all over my white blouse. Nora is startled by my reaction.

In the meantime, other children start entering the classroom. I tell her to go and read to herself and then I will read out loud to her. I quickly go to the staff toilets and clean my blouse.

Yuck, that child is filthy!

When I return, Nora is at my desk with the book. 'Are you going to read out loud now? May I sit next to you?' *She gets up on my office chair and I can smell her clothes and feel sick. I just can't sit next to this dirty child!*

Then Miss Marjan, the classroom teacher, walks in. 'Hello, Nora. Did your brother bring you to school again? It's a bit difficult for him to manage getting you washed and dressed, huh? Come with me to the toilet and we'll get you a fresh pair of underpants. Miss Karin will start with circle time soon'. *My cheeks burn: I should have thought of this myself.*

Reflecting on your own story

The use of the different lenses of students, colleagues, personal and theory for critical reflection (Brookfield, 2017) can be helpful when reflecting on your story.

Reflect on your own story using each of the following lenses.

Personal: examining our own experiences of learning to teach and how these may have unconsciously shaped our own practice.

- » Are there any reasons why I might have felt/behaved in this way?
- » Have I experienced anything similar in the past?
- » What are the values underpinning my practice here?
- » What does it reveal about the essence of who I am as a teacher?

Students: examining our students' perceptions and experiences of what we do in order to become aware of the impact of our actions and assumptions on relationships, dispositions and learning.

- » How did the student(s) involved experience this incident?
- » What impact did it have on our relationship?
- » What impact did it have on the students' attitudes?
- » What impact did it have on the students' learning?
- » How could I find out their perspective?
- » Would it be helpful to hear their perspective?

Colleagues: seeking our colleagues' perceptions and experiences of what we do, in order to illuminate aspects of our practice that are normally hidden, or to see them in a new light.

- » Who may provide me with a useful insight to this experience?
- » How will I invite their feedback?
- » Can I share my story with colleagues and allow them to ask me questions that help to reveal my assumptions?
- » Invite colleagues to give alternative interpretations of the events you describe.

Theory: engaging with theoretical frameworks and research in the literature, in pursuit of alternative interpretations of familiar situations. Reading theory can suggest different interpretations of familiar events and other ways of working.

- » Are there other ways of approaching this issue that I could investigate?
- » Can I find a useful book or article to help?
- » Is there anyone who can help to direct me towards alternative resources?

Each lens provides a different perspective from which to examine our practice. These can allow us to make sense of, and 'name', what we do, as well as providing mirrors to reflect back different versions of how our actions are received and interpreted by others.

Reflecting together on your stories of practice

The use of the 3D approach can be helpful when reflecting on stories of practice with colleagues or students (Graham, 2013).

Read the story, then:

» *discover* critical moments from practice in the story;

» *deepen* your understanding of the issues involved through asking open questions of the storywriter and linking with relevant literature;

» *do* set targets to make changes in practice to embed the new ideas.

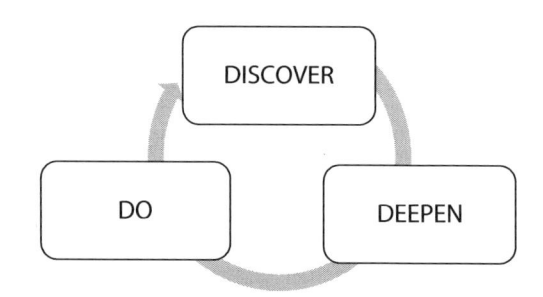

Discover	Deepen	Do
Create mutual openness and trust	Ask open questions	Identify next stages to take the learning forward
Be attentive and listen	Don't make assumptions	Establish a vision for the future
Show respect	Be non-judgemental	Set targets
Be patient and caring	Offer feedback through summarising, paraphrasing and further questioning	Critically reflect on insights gained and any new connections made
Create a positive environment	Make links between theory and practice	Identify patterns of behaviour
Show empathy	Share insights and hunches	Promote and support change
Exhibit a sense of sharing		Identify measures of success

(Graham, 2013, p 37)

REFLECTIONS

When we are looking at the stories about challenges in practice that have been written by those we are working alongside, in partnership, it will be important to draw on a coaching approach to giving feedback rather than a judgemental approach. Jarvis and Graham (2015) provide an example of how they made this explicit by using an approach they called 'It's not the Bake Off!' Judgements about quality from the perspective of the expert baker were compared to a coaching approach where the focus was to challenge the novice baker to think more deeply or differently and to identify their own solutions to issues.

References

Argyris, C and Schön, D (1974) *Theory in Practice: Increasing Professional Effectiveness*. San Francisco, CA: Jossey-Bass.

Brookfield, S D (2017) *Becoming a Critically Reflective Teacher.* 2nd ed. San Francisco, CA: Jossey-Bass.

Graham, S (2013) Enhancing Professional Learning Conversations. In White, E and Jarvis, J (eds) *School Based Teacher Training: A Handbook for Tutors and Mentors.* London: Sage.

Jarvis, J (2005) Telling Stories in Class: An Exploration of Aspects of the Use of Narrative in a Higher Education Context. *Journal for the Enhancement of Learning and Teaching*, 2(1): 6–13. [online] Available at: http://uhra.herts.ac.uk/handle/2299/2582 (accessed 6 February 2021).

Jarvis, J and Graham, S (2015) *Innovative Pedagogies Series: 'It's All About the Shoes' Exploring the Perspectives of Others and Ourselves in Teacher Education.* York: Higher Education Academy. [online] Available at: https://uhra.herts.ac.uk/bitstream/handle/2299/17319/joy_jarvis_final_templated_0.pdf?sequence=2 (accessed 6 February 2021).

Lewis, S, Passmore, J and Cantori, S (2011) *Appreciative Inquiry for Change Management: Using Appreciative Inquiry to Facilitate Organisational Development.* London: Kogan Press.

Mason, J (2002) *Researching Your Own Practice: The Discipline of Noticing*. London: Routledge.

Vokey, D and Kerr, J (2011) Intuition and Professional Wisdom: Can We Teach Moral Discernment? In Bondi, L, Carr, D, Clark, C and Clegg, C (eds) *Towards Professional Wisdom: Practical Deliberation in the People Professions.* Farnham: Ashgate Publishing.

CHAPTER 8 | USING THE STORIES CREATIVELY

KEY **THEMES**

This chapter is about:
- *additional ways of using the stories to support professional learning.*

How to use the stories

Each of the teacher educator stories has suggestions and ideas for your use of the story. Many of these different ideas have been contributed by the teacher educators taking part in workshops that we have run. You may decide that you would like to use a story in a different way, or to swap around the ways you use the stories. Table 8.1 provides ideas for ways to use the stories for your own workshops. We would be delighted to receive your further ideas for using stories for your professional development, and for collaborative professional learning with other teacher educators or stakeholders in initial teacher education.

Some of the stories might provide a useful stimulus for discussion about practice with your students, but students can also tell a wealth of stories about their experiences as they are learning teaching in these partnerships. Stories from students can also provide a rich resource for teacher educators to learn from. You may want to use writing stories about practice (from Chapter 7) with your students as an activity for their own reflection and professional development, individually or collaboratively, as well as for the professional learning of teacher educators and other stakeholders in your partnership. Jarvis and Iantaffi (2006) use a narrative approach with students to motivate them to engage with ideas about inclusion and, if necessary, to change their perspectives.

CRITICAL **QUESTIONS**

The stories in this handbook were written in response to the call to write a story about a challenge in practice that you are experiencing working 'on the ground' in partnerships. Another approach would be to carry out an appreciative inquiry (see Chapter 7) to collect stories of good practice, to further develop your partnership work.

» What prompts would you use?

Table 8.1 Some ways to use the stories

Suggestion of how to use the story	Story that uses this suggestion
Give the story a title Read through the story and identify the teacher educator's dilemma(s). What title would you give the story? Listen to the titles that others have given the story and why. Do you want to change the title that you have given the story? (None of the stories have been given titles because we noticed that different people will notice different things of importance to them within the stories. Providing a title could restrict the learning that you could get from them.)	All
Final thoughts Consider what you have learnt from the story and the activity. Share this with the group.	All
Resonance/dissonance Which parts of the story resonate with your experience and where is there dissonance?	2.1
Perspective taking Look at the story through the different perspectives of each of the participants – student, mentor, teacher educator, others… This can be done through sharing out the participants in your group, and then discussing together, hearing from each perspective.	2.2
Key words Highlight the significant words in the story for you. What does this show you about the story, and about you? How does this compare with what others felt was significant in the story?	2.3
Slicing After the challenge has been laid out, slice off the way that it was handled and discuss together ways that this situation could be handled. Then look at what the storyteller did.	3.1 and 3.2
Role playing Perspective taking can be developed further into taking on the roles of the different participants and exploring how you would respond to different ways to dealing with the challenge.	3.3

Table 8.1 (*Cont.*)

Suggestion of how to use the story	Story that uses this suggestion
Critical incident(s) Identify what you see as the critical incident in the story. What led up to this? What made it critical for the learning of the teacher educator? What learning can you get from this incident?	4.1
Identifying strategies What strategies were used by the teacher educator(s) in this story. How did this promote learning for the teacher educator and the student?	4.2
Positive feedback Consider how the participants in the story are feeling. What positive feedback would you give to the teacher educator(s) in the story? What positive feedback would you give to the student?	4.3
Key issue What do you think is the key issue in this story? Who is the key issue about? Why do you think you were drawn to this issue? How does this compare to the issues identified by others in your group?	5.1
Issues and outcomes What strikes you in this story, and what outcome is associated with that issue? What do you think about the outcome? Could it have been improved in any way for the participants in the story? Consider situations that you are aware of in which this issue has been a concern, and how it has been dealt with. Are there lessons to learn?	5.2
Dealing with the challenge What is the challenge in this story? Who is experiencing the challenge? Is it internal or external to the person? What suggestions can you each make towards dealing with this challenge? Decide together using these ideas what advice you would give to the teacher educator.	5.3
Words of wisdom From reading the story and discussing the challenge together, design a list of prompts that would provide 'words of wisdom' in similar situations.	

Table 8.1 (*Cont.*)

Suggestion of how to use the story	Story that uses this suggestion
Vision, values and beliefs What does the story reveal about the underlying beliefs and values of the teacher educator or the partnership? How do these compare to your own principles for teacher education, and those of your partnership?	
Discover, deepen, do In your group, one person shares their challenge or dilemma confidentially (*Discover*). Others ask them questions in order to understand more deeply, and to try and understand what is behind the issue (*Deepen*). The participants in pairs discuss possible answers and feed back to the group a summary of their thoughts and their proposal. The person who shared their challenge says which idea they will try and why (*Do*). Each person reflects on their own learning from the group session.	
Replying to an email If you got an email about this issue, what questions would you ask?	
In 2030… Read the story that is a current challenge. What caused the challenge? Where do you think we will be in five or ten years on this issue? Can it be solved? Does it need to be solved? If so, who should be involved in finding a solution?	
Exploring beliefs and values What issue is this story about? What have been your experiences with this issue? What do you think is most important about this issue? Why do you think this; what is your opinion based on (reading, practice, something else)? What is the most important next step for you in developing as a teacher educator? What is important to you about teacher educator development?	
A pathway for your personal and professional development as a teacher educator Looking at the issues that these stories have revealed, what implications do they have for your professional development as a teacher educator, and for your partnership? As a teacher educator, are there implications for developing your practice, identity and community? Are there things that you need to understand better about the context in which your partnership works? Are there things you need to understand better about the context within the partnership where you work?	

Reference

Jarvis, J and Iantaffi, A (2006) 'Deaf People Don't Dance': Challenging Student Teachers' Perspectives of Pupils and Inclusion. *Deafness & Education International*, 8(2): 75–87. https://doi.org/10.1179/146431506790560184

GLOSSARY

The terminology for the different participants in teacher education varies across providers and countries. The following table indicates what terms have been used in this handbook and, for guidance, what terms might be appropriate substitutes in your setting. When you are using the stories, you may find it helpful to make it clear at the beginning of the workshop what and who the terms refer to, and to identify the key people within your setting/partnership.

Table 9.1 Glossary of terms

Terms used in the resources	Alternative terms
Initial teacher education (ITE)	Initial teacher training (ITT)
School-based teacher educator (SBTE)	Professional mentor
	ITT supervisor
	ITT co-ordinator
	Senior link
	School-based trainer/tutor
Teacher mentor	Co-operating teacher
	School-based mentor
Student	Trainee
	Associate teacher
ITT/ITE provider	School-centred ITT (SCITT) provider
	School Direct partnership
	Higher education institution (HEI)
	Teacher education institute
	University

APPENDIX: LIST OF TEACHER EDUCATOR STORIES

Teacher educator story	Page	Corresponding FLiTE resource. Available at: www.go.herts.ac.uk/FLiTE
2.1	15	1
2.2	17	5
2.3	19	12
3.1	25	2
3.2	27	6
3.3	29	10
4.1	35	4
4.2	38	8
4.3	40	11
5.1	48	3
5.2	50	7
5.3	52	9

INDEX

3D approach (reflective practice), 70, 75

A

abbreviations, list of, viii
absences, dealing with, 19
affordance, 18–19, 47
ALGEE (mental health first aid), 42
appreciative inquiry, 66, 72
assessment, 3, 5, 13–16, 18–22, 35–8, 49, 52–3, 62

B

behaviour, 14, 43, 44
beliefs, 43, 75

C

challenges, in practice, 1, 2, 20, 21, 36, 37
    benefits of, x, 40
    cross-referenced with Mentor Standards, 61, 73
    informing curriculum design, 12
    narrative approach, 2–4, 25, 34, 47, 57–9, 66, 67–8
    reflections on, 43–4, 70
    subthemes of, 5
    and teacher education, 8–9, 48–9
change, impact of, 34–5, 60
classroom practice, 12, 13, 19, 61
coaching, 5, 7, 15, 18, 44, 46, 62, 70
    questions for, 21, 31, 42, 54, 64
cognitive dissonance, 58
collaboration, 5, 13, 24–32
    with IBTE communities, 2
    in partnerships, x, 3, 25–6, 43
    reflection on stories, 70
    use of critical questions, 7
    use of stories, 3, 6, 8, 57–65
colleagues, perspective of, 69
commitment, 27, 32, 33, 35
communication, 5, 26, 27–8, 29, 32
    through narrative, 2, 59
communities of practice, 58
competencies, 27, 36, 37, 43
confidence, 27, 30, 50, 62, 63
co-operation, 5, 25, 26, 28, 50, 62
creativity, in use of stories, 72, 73
critical incidents, x, 51, 55, 66, 74
curriculum, in ITE, 2, 8, 12–13, 17, 21–2, 43, 59–60

D

data, student access to, 17, 18
dilemmas, dealing with, 73, 75
    in assessment, 13, 15
    in ITE, 1, 17, 18
    in partnerships, 4, 25, 28
Discover, Deepen, Do (3D approach), 70, 75
dissonance, 16, 58, 73
diversity, 55, 61
    of pupil population, 2

E

England, 1, 2, 3–4, 12, 42, 61
environment
    in onion model, 43
    see also landscapes (educational)
equality, 12, 61
ethos, 35
evaluation, 47
evidence-based practice, 2, 54
expectations, 34
    of schools, 2, 25
    of students, 13, 30, 31, 50, 63
    of teachers/teacher educators, 33

F

feedback, 70, 75
    from colleagues, 69
    and identity, 34
    mentor training, 6
    positive, 53, 74
    for students, 15, 20, 46, 50, 52, 61, 62
FLiTE (For Learning in Teacher Education), x, 78

G

glossary, 77
Graham, S, 57, 67, 70
growth
    see personal and professional growth
guidance, 54, 58

H

Hallett, F, 51
higher education institution (HEI), 77
    see also initial teacher education (ITE): partnerships

I

Iantaffi, A, 72
identity, as teachers, 33–4, 43
    link with practice, 58–9
InFo-TED, 9, 55
initial teacher education (ITE), viii, x, 2, 3, 77
    challenges in, ix, 1, 3, 8
    curriculum development, 12–13, 21, 43, 59
    partnerships, x, 24, 32, 44, 47, 58–9, 75
    policy, 18, 43
    quality assurance, 47
    research literacy in, 13, 54
    stories, use of, ix
    support in, 46
    well-being of stakeholders, 35
initial teacher training (ITT)
    see initial teacher education (ITE)
institute-based teacher educators (IBTEs), 1, 4
    changing roles of, 2
    current research focus on, x
    and the Mentor Standards, 61
    responsibilities of, 3
    in stories, 5, 17, 18, 19, 25–6, 28, 35, 37, 38, 49
interventions, at different levels, 44
ITT co-ordinator/supervisor
    see school-based teacher educators (SBTEs)
ITT Core Content Framework, 12, 59

J

Jarvis, J, 57, 67, 70, 72
judgementoring, 21

K

key words, use of, 73
Korsgaard, M T, 2

L

landscapes (educational), 9, 24, 34, 35
Lave, J, 34
leadership, 7, 8, 9, 32, 60–1
    working with, 5
lenses, 69

M

management, 25, 32, 38, 47, 61
McAteer, M, 51
mental health, 1, 6, 35, 40–1, 42, 63
    first aid, 41–2, 44
mentor, professional
    see school-based teacher educators (SBTEs)
Mentor Standards, 61, 73
mentoring, 46–7
    conflict with assessor role, 13
    development through stories, 61
    ensuring access to learning opportunities, 47
    mentoring the mentors, 47
    quality assurance of, 52–3
    relationship difficulties, 50, 63
    training for mentors, 48–9, 63
    use of coaching questions, 7
Mutton, T, 21, 47, 59, 60
Mynott, J P, 58

N

narrative approach, x, 1, 2, 8, 9
    see also stories
National Association of School-Based Teacher Trainers (NASBTT), 9, 55
National Standards, 46, 61
Netherlands, the, 3, 4
newly qualified teachers (NQTs), ix, 19

O

'onion model', the, 43–4
outcomes, 74

P

partnerships, 9, 24
    culture of, 58
    vision for, 60
pedagogy, 1, 2, 13, 52
personal and professional growth, 2, 6, 39–40, 43
personal identity, 34
policy, 14, 22, 33, 54, 59
    for ITE, 18, 43
practitioner research, 54
pregnancy, dealing with, 19
problems, dealing with, 14, 21, 37–8, 63
professional identity, 33
professional inquiry, 54
professional learning and development, ix, 6, 7, 47, 57, 66
    communities in, x, 2, 43, 47

evidence-based practice, 58
individual and collaborative, 8
international context of, 8
narrative approach to, x, 1
responsibility for, 1–2, 3
stories as tools for, 3, 4, 8, 57–8, 61, 72
in students, 12, 21, 59
for teacher educators, ix, x, 4, 8, 34, 46, 51, 54
professional mentors
    see school-based teacher educators (SBTEs)
professionalism, 6, 46
    students, 33
    teacher educators, 33–4
progress, assisting students with, 16
prompts, for reflection, 51
purpose, 44, 60

Q

quality
    of provision, x, 6, 17, 18, 21, 46
    quality assurance, 3, 6, 13, 47, 54

R

randomised controlled trials (RCTs), 2
reflections, 7, 9, 13, 15–16, 34, 62
    challenges, 43–4
    ITE partnerships, 32
    on own stories about practice, 67, 68–70
    prompts for, 51
    quality of provision, 21
    research and professional inquiry, 54–5
    schools role in ITE, 8–9
    third space, 64–5
relationships
    mentor–mentee, 50
    time requirement for, 35
research, 54
resilience, 9, 34–5, 39, 44, 60
resonance, 16, 73
responsibilities
    of students, 37
    of teacher educators, 3, 34
role play, 29, 73
roles, changing nature of, 2

S

safeguarding, 43
School Direct partnerships, 3
    see also initial teacher education (ITE): partnerships
school-based teacher educators (SBTEs), viii, 1–2, 4
    changing roles of, 2, 8
    glossary, 77

and the Mentor Standards, 61
    research focus on, x
    responsibilities of, 3, 47–9
    in stories, 5, 15, 18, 19, 27–8, 29, 50, 52
    working in partnership with, 25–6
school-based trainer/tutors
    see school-based teacher educators (SBTEs)
school-centred ITT (SCITT) provider
    see initial teacher education (ITE): partnerships
senior link role
    see school-based teacher educators (SBTEs)
situated identity, 34
slicing (story analysis), 73
social media, issues with, 39
staff rooms, 18, 25, 38
stakeholders, 3, 9, 22, 57, 60, 72
    perspectives on practice, x, 13, 24, 32, 47, 57, 60
    terminology, 3
    well-being of, 35
standards
    reliance on, 29
stories
    benefits of using, x, 2–3, 12, 13, 25, 34, 44
    collaborative use of, 57–9
    collection process, 3–4
    cross-referenced with National Standards, 61
    curriculum design, 59–60
    ideas for use, 6–7, 8–9, 72–3
    leadership development, 60–1
    mentor development, 61
    quality assurance process, 47
    themes and subthemes, 5
    writing your own, 66–70
storytelling, 2
strategies, 3, 16, 40, 42, 50, 53, 61, 74
students
    access to learning opportunities, 17, 47, 62
    perspective of, 69
    responsibilities of, 37
    supporting, 62

T

teacher education institute
    see initial teacher education (ITE): partnerships
Teacher Educator and Mentoring Zone (TEMZ), 9, 55
teacher educators
    beliefs about roles, 34
    definition, 1
    influencing identity, 34
    professional learning, x, 1–2
    see also institute-based teacher educators (IBTEs); school-based teacher educators (SBTEs)
teacher mentors
    see school-based teacher educators (SBTEs)

INDEX

teacher retention, 2
Teachers' Standards (DfE), 14
tensions, 6, 24, 33, 34, 61
terminology, use of, 58, 77
themes/subthemes of stories, 4, 5
theory, 54
    examining stories through lens of, 69
third spaces (for knowledge sharing), 25, 32, 64
titles of stories, as learning tool, 3, 31, 73

U

universities
    see initial teacher education (ITE): partnerships

V

values, 60, 69, 75
    and resilience, 35
vision, 35, 37, 60, 70, 75
visiting tutors, 7

W

well-being, 1, 6, 35, 41, 43
    of students, 33
Wenger, E, 34
workload, 35
workshops, 8, 57–8, 72, 77
writing (your own stories about practice), 66–70